Learning to use statistical tests in psychology

SECOND EDITION

Learning to use statistical tests in psychology

SECOND EDITION

**Judith Greene
and
Manuela d'Oliveira**

Open University Press
Buckingham · Philadelphia

Open University Press
Celtic Court
22 Ballmoor
Buckingham
MK18 1XW

email: enquiries@openup.co.uk
world wide web: http://www.openup.co.uk

and
325 Chestnut Street
Philadelphia, PA 19106, USA

First published 1982
Reprinted 1983, 1985, 1987, 1988, 1989, 1990, 1992, 1993, 1994, 1995, 1996, 1998

First published in this second edition, 1999
Reprinted 2000

A catalogue record of this book is available from the British Library

ISBN   0 335 20378 7 (hb)   0 335 20377 9 (pb)

Library of Congress Cataloging-in-Publication Data
Greene, Judith.
    Learning to use statistical tests in psychology/Judith Greene
and Manuela d'Oliveira. – 2nd ed.
        p.   cm. – (Open guides to psychology)
    Includes bibliographical references and index.
    ISBN 0-335-20378-7 (hardcover). – ISBN 0-335-20377-9 (pbk.)
    1. Research methods.   2. Psychology – Statistical methods.
I. D'Oliveira, Manuela.   II. Title.   III. Series.
BF39.G725   1999
150′.7′27–dc21   99-13094
                                                                           CIP

Typeset by Graphicraft Ltd, Hong Kong
Printed in Great Britain by St Edmundsbury Press Ltd, Bury St Edmunds, Suffolk

To Norman, Kate and Matthew
and
To Eduardo

Contents

Part II   Non-parametric tests

Part III   Parametric tests

Preface to the second edition

There have been an enormous number of textbooks which have claimed to present statistics in a simple way. Despite this, many psychology students still find the whole statistical business something of a mystery.

How does this book differ from these other attempts?

We believe that virtually all books on statistics feel obliged to start with the mathematical principles underlying probability distributions, samples and populations, and statistical testing. But, however simply these are presented, in our view they obscure the basic reasons why psychologists use statistical tests.

So we had better come clean straight away. This book sets out to achieve one single aim. This is to enable students to select appropriate statistical tests to evaluate the significance of data obtained from psychological experiments. In other words, this book is concerned with *inferential statistics* as used in psychological experimental studies.

We have concentrated on this to the exclusion of much else. Topics like descriptive statistics and the basic principles of probability are well covered in other statistical texts. Moreover, we will be concentrating on psychological *experiments* rather than other types of psychological investigation. There is nothing here about the use of surveys, observational techniques or psychometric tests of intelligence and personality. All we have included is the battery of statistical tests which are usually introduced to psychology students as part of their undergraduate laboratory course. We hope that, by aiming at a single target, we will maximize our chances of scoring a bull's-eye.

While this is definitely a 'beginners' book, it takes students from the simplest non-parametric tests, like the Wilcoxon test, through to complex analysis of variance designs. The principle is the same throughout: always to give the rationale for using appropriate statistical analyses for particular experimental designs. It is certainly our expectation that anyone who has mastered the why and how of the statistical tests given in this book will be in a position to understand the basic principles of statistical tests as presented in advanced textbooks of psychological statistics.

Our belief is that, with the aid of this book, students will feel comfortable about the basis for selecting and applying all kinds of statistical tests. We hope that teachers will wish to use a book which frees students from much of the panic usually associated with statistics. That way they should be in a far more receptive state to learn.

The major change in the second edition is that the book is now organized into three parts. Part I contains a general introduction to the principles of research and design. Part II presents all the information required for non-parametric tests. It is not until Part III that multivariable designs are introduced to prepare students for analysis of variance.

We hope this reorganization will have several advantages. Both students and teachers will gain from the clear division between non-parametric and parametric tests. The new approach embraces the principle of introducing more complex designs on a 'need to know' basis, providing room for a more extended treatment of concepts students find difficult, like degrees of freedom and interactions.

The second innovation is to introduce students to the use of computerized statistics packages. Although many readers will have access to computer programs, we still provide step-by-step instructions for those who do not. One danger is that when students can simply press buttons on a computer they can lose sight of the purpose of statistical analysis. We have concentrated on ensuring that students understand the inputs and can interpret the outputs of programs.

This book does not attempt to provide complete instructions for logging into particular packages, all of which differ slightly. A brief account is given in Appendix 1 about one of the most commonly used computer packages and the appropriate terminology. The intention is that students will have no problem in adapting easily to whichever programs are available in a particular institution.

Note about subjects and participants

Traditionally psychologists used the word 'subjects' to describe the people taking part in experiments in order to distinguish them from 'objects'. More recently, it has been agreed by the British Psychological Society that a better term would be 'participants' in order to remind researchers that people are participating in their experiments. However, it is not common to use this term when describing experimental designs and statistics. For instance, 'within-participants' and 'between-participants' would sound quite odd, rather than the usual 'between-subjects' and 'within-subjects'.

The usage in this book refers to the *people* taking part in experiments and the differences between people as a source of variability. But, when the discussion from Chapter 2 onwards moves to types of experimental designs and the consequences of using same and different subjects, 'subjects' is used in its technical sense (as in the Decision Charts).

Study guide for students

The aim of this book is to explain the rationale for using statistical tests to evaluate the results of psychological experiments. The problem is that in psychology you have to carry out these experiments on *human beings*, often other students. Unlike most physical objects, human beings are unique, each interpreting and performing whatever task you set them in a slightly different way.

You will find that the data and observations obtained from the people doing a psychological experiment are often extremely varied and that many of the things which influence their behaviour may have nothing to do with the experiment. It is for this reason that you have to sort out whether experimental results are really significant. And, as you will see, this is just what statistical tests enable you to do.

You will probably be relieved to hear that the chapters which introduce the basic rationale for statistics and summarize all you need to know in order to select an appropriate statistical test are the shortest chapters in the book. These are aspects of using statistical tests that students often find rather puzzling, but we hope that these chapters will clear up all your worries.

Other chapters in the book present statistical tests, explaining the rationale for each one, taking you 'step by step' through any necessary calculations and giving precise instructions about how to use the statistical tables in Appendix 2. For more complex types of statistical analysis you will be introduced to the latest types of computer programs for carrying out numerical calculations.

One essential feature of this book is the *questions* which occur throughout the text. It is not enough to read the summaries presented in the *progress boxes*. The only way you can make sure that you understand the context of each section is to attempt the questions *before* looking up the answers at the back! It is equally important to work your way through the step-by-step instructions given for each statistical test. Otherwise, you will never gain the confidence which comes from fully understanding the rationale for a statistical test as you successfully complete the necessary arithmetical calculations.

Let us end by making some important, and, we hope, encouraging points. The first thing to grasp is that statistical tests are not magic formulae to be turned to, desperately wondering which on earth to choose. They simply follow as a natural result of the kind of experiment you have chosen to do. What makes most people give up all hope of mastering statistics is the thought that they will find themselves presented with a huge amount of numerical data without the foggiest idea of how to deal with them. But this is quite the wrong way to go about things. The important thing is to decide what experiment you want to carry out. You will find that such a decision immediately narrows your possible choice of statistical tests to only one or two, and that there are good reasons for selecting one or the other.

With statistical tests selection is all; the actual calculations are quite easy once you have understood the reasons for doing them. The aim has been to introduce the principles of using statistical tests *without referring to any mathematical concepts*. And, in order to do the calculations for the tests themselves, you will only need to know how to add, subtract, multiply, divide and square numbers. With modern pocket calculators and computer programs this really should be child's play.

Good luck – and if, in spite of everything, you do find yourself getting disheartened by statistics, turn back and reread this study guide.

Acknowledgements

Grateful acknowledgement is made to the following sources for permission to reprint the tables in this book:

Table A from F. Wilcoxon and R.A. Wilcox, *Some Rapid Approximate Statistical Procedures*, American Cyanamid Co., 1949;

Table B from R.P. Runyon and A. Haber, *Fundamentals of Behavioral Statistics*, 3rd edn, Reading, Mass., Addison-Wesley, 1976;

Table C from M. Friedman, 'The use of ranks to avoid the assumption of normality implicit in the analysis of variance' in *Journal of the American Statistical Association*, Vol. 32, 1937;

Table D from E.E. Page's article in *Journal of the American Statistical Association*, Vol. 58, 1963;

Table E from W.H. Kruskal and W.A. Wallis, 'Use of ranks in one-criterion variance analysis' in *Journal of the American Statistical Association*, Vol. 47, 1952;

Table F from D.V. Lindley and J.C.P. Miller, *Cambridge Elementary Statistical Tables*, 10th edn, Cambridge University Press, 1973;

Table G from A.R. Jonckheere, 'A distribution-free k-sample test against ordered alternatives' in *Biometrika*, Vol. 41, Biometrika Trustees, 1954;

Table H from E.G. Olds, 'The 5% significance levels for sums of squares of rank differences and a correction' in *Annals of Mathematical Statistics*, Vol. 20, Institute of Mathematical Statistics, 1949;

Table I from D.V. Lindley and J.C.P. Miller, *Cambridge Elementary Statistical Tables*, 10th edn, Cambridge University Press, 1973;

Table J from D.V. Lindley and J.C.P. Miller, *Cambridge Elementary Statistical Tables*, 10th edn, Cambridge University Press, 1973.

Prologue

The way we propose to tackle the daunting task of introducing statistics 'without tears' is to concentrate on what statistical tests are *for*. Once you have grasped this we hope the rest will fall into place.

The first thing to consider is *why* psychologists carry out experiments. The simple answer is that they want to develop and test *theories* about human nature and experience.

Let us start by supposing that you as a psychologist have a theory about how children acquire reading skills. On the basis of this you have developed a new reading scheme which consists of a set of picture/sentence cards. Now you want to carry out some research to demonstrate whether your theory works or not. Filled with enthusiasm, you find a friendly school which allows you to give your reading scheme to a group of children and to measure their reading scores at the end of term. What might be the reaction of a sceptical teacher?

Sceptical teacher: How do I know the children's scores were any better after the reading scheme than they were before?

You as a researcher: Well, I measured their reading scores *before* as well as *after* the reading scheme. Their scores after the scheme were higher, showing an improvement in reading.

Sceptic: Can you be sure that their scores wouldn't have gone up anyway without the scheme? After all, the children were 3 months older by the time you tested them the second time.

Researcher: I compared the reading scores of the children who were given the reading scheme with another group of children who didn't have the scheme. The children who were given the scheme improved more.

Sceptic: How do you know that the children you gave the reading scheme to weren't better at reading anyway? Or perhaps they were worse at reading in the first place and so had more room for improvement. Or perhaps the first lot were all girls who tend to learn to read more quickly.

Researcher: I tried to match my two groups of children as carefully as possible for all relevant factors, e.g. sex, intelligence, initial reading skills. As it wouldn't have been possible to match the children on all possible characteristics, I otherwise allocated them randomly to the two groups. So any differences between the groups ought to be due to my reading scheme rather than to any other factor.

Sceptic: How can you be sure that the teacher who administered the reading scheme wasn't particularly enthusiastic about it and expected improved reading scores? The other group may have got the same old bored and discouraged teacher and that's why their scores didn't go up – nothing to do with your reading scheme.

Researcher: I was particularly careful that the same teacher was responsible for teaching both groups and that he/she was given something interesting to do even with the other group of children.

Sceptic: But if you only used one teacher at one school how do I know that your reading scheme would help children in other schools?

Researcher: What I really meant to say was that I carried out the research in several schools, all in different areas and with different kinds of children.

Sceptic: How did you manage to standardize conditions in all these different schools, or did you let things just happen?

Researcher: I made up some instructions telling teachers how to administer the reading tests, how many weeks to operate the scheme, how large the classes should be, and so on.

Sceptic: The more I hear you talking the more I wonder about all the variability introduced by using different children, different teachers, different schools. Individuals vary so much in their performance, even from day to day. How can you be certain that the improvement in reading scores that you attribute to your reading scheme is big enough to count as a real difference between the reading scheme group and the no reading scheme group? Perhaps the results of your experiment were all due to chance fluctuations in performance.

Researcher: Ah well, I went off and did a statistical test which told me that the difference in reading scores between the two groups was unlikely to have occurred simply by chance. It was a big enough and a consistent enough difference to count as a real difference between the two groups of children.

Sceptic: Now I come to think of it, I am not really interested in overall differences between children who were given the reading scheme and those who were not. What I want to know is whether it is only children who are fairly good at spelling who benefit from the scheme, or whether it is particularly helpful for backward spellers.

Researcher: Why didn't you say so before? I could have measured the children's initial spelling scores to see whether it was children with less good or better spelling scores who were most likely to show improvement after the reading scheme.

Sceptic: But, even if you found that better spelling scores were associated with improved reading scores, mightn't this be due to some quite different factor? Children who enjoy school lessons may be more likely both to be good spellers and to benefit from any new teaching scheme? So it wouldn't be spelling ability as such which was responsible for these children showing more improvement.

Researcher: It certainly is a problem to discover exactly what lies behind an association between spelling and reading scores. That is why it would be a good idea to have equal numbers of less good and good spellers, and children who enjoy and who hate school lessons in my experiment. That way I might be able to find out whether spelling abilities or attitudes to school have an effect on whether children benefit from the reading scheme.

In this Prologue we have raised some possible objections to experimental research. A lot of them stem from the fact that psychologists study people rather than physical objects. The trouble with people from a psychologist's point of view is that they differ from each other in so many unpredictable ways. Of course, from the point of view of the people themselves, they are pleased that there is so much variability in people's behaviour.

So what is the unfortunate researcher to do? Obviously it is not possible to look at all possible factors which might affect the way children learn to read. Sometimes it is appropriate for psychologists to carry out an exploratory investigation in which they can observe as much as they can about ongoing behaviour. This can be a useful stage in developing a theory about what might be the most important factors affecting a particular type of behaviour. However, at some point a researcher will want to test out a theory. In order to do this, the researcher will make a prediction about the kind of behaviour which would be expected to occur if the theory is true.

Part I   Introduction

1 Introduction to experimental research

1.1 The experimental hypothesis

The aim of psychological research is to test psychological theories. Researchers make predictions which would arise from a theory and design an experiment to see whether the results support the prediction or not. This may be clearer from an example. Suppose the theory is that words are remembered as whole words rather than as groups of letters. The prediction would be that all words are equally easy to remember, long words like *catapult* being as easy as *cat*, rare words like *anteater* as easy as common words like *elephant*. The test would be to carry out an experiment to find out whether people actually find all these words equally easy to recall.

In experimental research a prediction is formulated as an experimental hypothesis. It is called a hypothesis because it is not known until after the experiment has been done whether the prediction is supported or not. So the prediction is only a hypothesis, i.e. something which is proposed and has to be tested.

An **experimental hypothesis** makes a *prediction* about the effects of one or more events on people's behaviour. For instance, a researcher may predict that being given a reading scheme will improve reading skills. The aim of an experiment is to test whether the experimental hypothesis is supported by the behaviour of the people who are taking part in the experiment.

1.2 The null hypothesis

One especially important point to note is that in order to test an experimental hypothesis it must be possible for the predicted effects to occur or *not* to occur. If it were always certain that the predicted behaviour would occur there would be no point in doing an experiment. In our example, it must be possible for the results of the reading scheme either to *support* the experimental hypothesis (i.e. that children given the reading scheme will obtain higher reading scores) or *not* to support the hypothesis (i.e. that there will be no differences in reading scores between the children whether they are given the reading scheme or not).

This is a basic rule of experimental research. An experimental hypothesis is always tested against a **null hypothesis**, which states that an experimenter will *not* find the experimental results he/she expects. According to the null hypothesis, any results found in an experiment are due to random fluctuations in people's performance rather than the predicted effects the experimenter is interested in.

The next question is how to set about showing whether there is indeed a predicted relationship between two events (i.e. whether the reading scheme versus no reading scheme has any effect on children's reading scores). In other words, how can we rule out the null hypothesis?

1.3   Independent and dependent variables

An experimental hypothesis predicts a relationship between two events. One would be the event of being exposed to a reading scheme and the other the event of measuring children's reading scores. In research, these events are usually called **variables** because the events can vary. This applies to the variable which the researcher manipulates, for example, presenting a reading scheme or not presenting a reading scheme. It also applies to the scores which the subjects produce. Obviously children's reading scores vary over a wide range – in fact it would be strange if reading scores were all the same.

We should now like to introduce the terminology of independent variables and dependent variables. The variable which the researcher manipulates is known as the **independent variable**. This is because the experimental conditions to test this variable are set up *independently* before the experiment even begins. The second variable, representing children's scores, is known as the **dependent variable**. This is because the reading scores are *dependent* on the way in which the experimenter manipulates the independent variable of the reading scheme.

The most common method of testing variables in a psychological experiment is for the experimenter to manipulate an *independent variable* to see whether it has an effect on the *dependent variable*. In the reading scheme experiment the researcher manipulates one variable (reading scheme or no reading scheme) to see what effect this will have on another variable (children's reading scores). If children who are given the reading scheme show more improvement in reading scores than children given no reading scheme, then the experimenter could claim that the relationship between the two variables was in the direction predicted by the experimental hypothesis, namely that the reading scheme would improve children's reading skills.

The basic experimental design is to allocate people to **experimental conditions** representing different conditions for the independent variable (reading scheme versus no reading scheme). In this way a comparison can be made between the experimental conditions to see what effect manipulating the reading scheme variable has on the dependent variable of reading scores.

? Question 1   Suppose a psychologist designs an experiment to test an experimental hypothesis that people will take less time to read a text with illustrations than the same text without illustrations.

(a) What is the independent variable?

(b) What is the dependent variable?

(c) What is the experimental hypothesis?

(d) What is the null hypothesis?

(Answers on p. 176)

(Answers on p. 176)

1.4 Controlling irrelevant variables

It is important to grasp that the point of designing an experiment is to demonstrate that the results are due to the independent variable selected by the researcher *and to nothing else*. Any other variable that may be affecting subjects' behaviour is considered undesirable. Such variables are called **irrelevant variables** because they are irrelevant to the main purpose of an experiment. For instance, suppose a researcher is interested in investigating the effect of a reading scheme. From this point of view, the motivation of teachers is an irrelevant variable which might be affecting children's performance in unpredictable ways.

The fact that teachers who present the reading scheme may be more motivated and enthusiastic would still result in the predicted effect that the children with the reading scheme would show improved performance. But the result might be due to the irrelevant variable that the children had a more interesting teacher. The experimenter intended to test the effects of the reading scheme, not the irrelevant variable of enthusiastic versus boring teachers.

It is possible for an experimenter to take action about an irrelevant variable as long as he/she realizes that it could be a possible alternative explanation of the children's behaviour. For instance, the researcher could make sure that equally good teachers were selected for both the reading scheme and the no reading scheme groups and that the teacher gave an interesting class to the no reading scheme group. In this way, the potentially irrelevant variable of enthusiastic versus boring teachers would have been systematically eliminated.

Good experimenters attempt to develop **standardized experimental procedures** by specifying the instructions to be given to subjects, the location and the timing of the experiment. The written and spoken materials to be used in the reading scheme and the measure of reading scores will all have been decided in advance. The objective is to eliminate as many irrelevant variables as possible.

Another type of irrelevant variable is caused by individual variability which affects people's performance. Some of the children may have parents who don't care about school, others may believe that their reading performance is already excellent, others may be daydreaming or looking out of the window. It would be very difficult for the experimenter to make allowance for all these kinds of irrelevant variables. It might be possible to take into account parents' attitudes to school as an extra independent variable. But things would get out of hand if any systematic attempt was made to control irrelevant variables like daydreaming. The researcher has to live with this kind of individual variability.

The truth of the matter is that it is impossible to control all irrelevant variables which may influence people's behaviour. It is for this reason that researchers employ statistical tests to test the effects of predicted independent variables against all other potential irrelevant variables.

 Progress box one

Relations between variables

- An *experimental hypothesis* predicts a relationship between variables.
- *Variables* are any characteristics which vary in an experimental situation.
- The experimenter manipulates *independent variables* and predicts their effects on *dependent variables*.
- The experimenter sets up *experimental conditions* in which an independent variable is varied (e.g. reading scheme versus no reading scheme). The scores represent *differences* in the dependent variable (e.g. reading scores) between the people allocated to the experimental conditions.

- The *null hypothesis* states that the scores resulting from an experiment are not due to the effects of an independent variable as predicted by the experimental hypothesis. Instead people's scores are influenced by the effects of *irrelevant variables*.
- Experimenters attempt to *standardize* experimental procedures in order to eliminate irrelevant variables.
- It is impossible to *eliminate* all individual variability.

2 Introduction to experimental design

2.1 Experimental and control conditions

As discussed in Chapter 1, the aim of experimental research is to vary the independent variable and predict its effects on the dependent variable of people's scores. The basic experimental design is for the researcher to allocate people to **experimental conditions** representing the independent variable. A comparison is made between people's scores on the dependent variable depending on which experimental conditions they have been allocated to. For instance, children would be allocated to a reading scheme condition or a no reading scheme condition and their reading scores would be measured.

Suppose a researcher has an experimental hypothesis which predicts that a reading scheme will improve children's reading scores.

Do you think it would be a sufficient test of this hypothesis to give a group of children the reading scheme and then to measure their reading scores?

How would the researcher know whether the children's reading scores were any higher than they would have been if they had been given no reading scheme at all? One way of dealing with this is to give the children a reading test *before* the reading scheme and then another test *afterwards* to see whether their scores had improved. The experimental design would look like this:

Test 1 Pre-test reading scores	*Experimental condition* Reading scheme	*Test 2* Post-test reading scores

Suppose the researcher found that the children's reading scores were higher on the post-test than on the pre-test. Could he/she be sure that the improvement in reading scores from pre-test to post-test was caused by the reading scheme?

Even if there were an improvement in scores it might have occurred in any case, either because the children were that much older, or because of all the other changes which might have happened to them between the two tests, e.g. a new teacher had arrived, and it was this change that had increased their reading scores. The only way to discover whether any improvement in scores is due to the intended independent variable is to design an experiment in which the *only* difference between conditions is whether children have been given the reading scheme or not.

It is for this reason that experimental designs often introduce a **control condition** against which the effects of an independent variable can be compared. The point about a control condition is that it is a condition in which people are *not* subjected to the experimental condition. So it is possible to compare two conditions, one *with* the reading scheme and one *without* the reading scheme. The experimental design would be:

Experimental condition
Pre-test scores   Reading scheme   Post-test scores

Control condition
Pre-test scores   No reading scheme   Post-test scores

The prediction would be that there would be more improvement in the post-test reading scores for the experimental condition than for the control condition. With this design the researcher might indeed find some improvement in scores for both conditions due to other variables such as growing older or new teachers. However, if there were a significantly *greater* improvement in the experimental condition, it can be claimed that this extra improvement is due, not to natural changes which might have affected both conditions equally, but to the reading scheme which affected only the experimental condition and not the control condition.

Sometimes, rather than comparing an experimental and a control condition, it is more appropriate to compare two levels of an independent variable. An example would be an experiment to investigate whether lists of common words are easier to remember than lists of rare words. The experimental design would simply compare memory scores under two experimental conditions:

Experimental condition 1
Learning lists of common words

Experimental condition 2
Learning lists of rare words

Question 2   Suppose the researcher was testing a theory that common words are more easily accessed in memory than rare words.

(a) What would the experimental hypothesis predict?

(b) What is the null hypothesis?

(c) Specify two experimental conditions for common words and rare words.

(d) What is the dependent variable?

(e) Would higher recall scores in experimental condition 1 support the experimental hypothesis?

2.2   Three or more experimental conditions

So far we have been talking about comparing only *two* experimental conditions. But you might want to look at more than two conditions to test an independent variable. For instance, you might be interested in whether different reading schemes would have different effects on children's reading scores. So you might like to compare the effects of reading scheme A and reading scheme B. You would still probably feel that it would be a good idea to have a control condition with no reading scheme. So the experimental design would have *three* conditions as follows:

Experimental condition 1
Pre-test scores   Reading scheme A   Post-test scores

Experimental condition 2
Pre-test scores   Reading scheme B   Post-test scores

Control condition
Pre-test scores   No reading scheme   Post-test scores

You would still be testing the independent variable (reading schemes) but that independent variable would have **three conditions** (two experimental conditions and one control condition). The prediction would be that there will be differences in scores between the three conditions.

Rather than just looking at overall differences between the three conditions, you might want to predict that the effect of the three levels would show a **trend**, predicting least improvement in the no reading scheme condition, an intermediate amount of improvement for reading scheme B and most improvement for reading scheme A.

? **Question 3** Consider an experiment with three experimental conditions, learning lists of very common words, less common words and words which occur very rarely.

(a) List three experimental conditions for this experiment.

(b) What hypothesis might the experimenter predict between memory scores for the three experimental conditions?

2.3 Different subjects (unrelated designs)

We introduced the problem of variability in the people who are acting as subjects in an experiment. One important consideration is whether it is better to use *different* subjects in each experimental condition or whether the *same* people should act as subjects in all experimental conditions.

We will first discuss the pros and cons of using different groups of subjects in each experimental condition. There are many experiments when it is essential to use different people for each experimental condition. Think again about the research into reading schemes.

Imagine that you were interested in whether boys or girls were more likely to benefit from the reading scheme. There is simply no way in which the same children could be allocated to both the boys' and the girls' groups. So there would obviously have to be different children in the two groups. The same would apply if you wanted to look at differences between good and bad spellers. At any given moment people are either good or bad at spelling and so *different* subjects would have to be allocated to the good and bad spelling groups.

This kind of experimental design is known as a **between-subjects** or **unrelated design** because the comparison is between two groups of subjects whose scores are *unrelated*.

What would be the advantages of having groups of different children in the reading scheme condition and the no reading scheme condition?

The main advantage is that each of the children would come new to each condition. Imagine that the same children were first given a reading scheme and then later a no reading scheme condition. The effects of doing the reading scheme first would obviously affect the way they would perform in the condition when they were later supposed to have no reading scheme. Using different subjects is always the best option when one experimental condition may have an effect on another experimental condition.

There are other cases when it is easier to use different groups of subjects. For instance, there are experiments which may depend on, at least temporarily, misleading people about the true purpose of the experiment.

To take an example, people may be asked to look at a list of words and put them into certain categories. Then they are suddenly asked to remember the words when they were not expecting to. This kind of experiment depends on people not knowing about the memory task beforehand. You could not use the same people more than once because the second time round they would already know that you were going to spring a 'surprise' memory task on them.

So far we have been talking about the advantages of using different subjects. But there is one crucial disadvantage of using different groups of subjects. Being different people, they are likely to differ in their reactions to each experimental condition. Some people might think the experiment a bore, some might not even be able to read, some might be old, some young, some might be planning their next holiday, and others might have forgotten their spectacles. As a result of all these individual differences, people's performance might be affected by irrelevant variables which have nothing to do with the independent variable the experimenter is intending to manipulate.

Researchers attempt to deal with the individual variability arising from using different subjects in two main ways. The first is to try and *match* the groups of subjects in each condition. The researcher might give subjects a memory test and make sure that groups of subjects in the two experimental conditions contain the same number of good and not so good memorizers. Or, if age is likely to influence the results, equal numbers of older and younger subjects would be allocated to the two conditions.

Often it is not possible to match for individual variability, for instance, whether people daydream or concentrate. The only way of dealing with this kind of individual variability is to allocate different people at random to experimental conditions. Here *random* means that it is purely a matter of *chance* which people end up doing which condition. The reasoning is that if subjects are randomly allocated to experimental conditions, then people of different ages or abilities are just as likely to be found in all the experimental groups. For example, you might find that all the subjects who arrive first to volunteer for an experiment are the most highly motivated people who tend to score more highly, quite regardless of experimental condition. So they should not be placed in the same group. It would be better to allocate alternate subjects as they arrive, or perhaps to toss a coin to decide the group for each subject. In this case, the allocation of subjects to groups should be truly random.

To sum up, there are many good reasons for using different groups of subjects, the most important of which is that no subject has to do more than one condition. This means that they are not influenced by having had to do something else before. The major disadvantage is that there will be extra variability because different groups of people may vary individually in all sorts of unexpected ways.

2.4   Same subjects (related designs)

From the point of view of eliminating individual differences, there is an even better experimental design than random allocation of different subjects. This is to use the *same* subjects for all experimental conditions. The point is that anything peculiar to one individual (like high or low motivation or age) is the same across all conditions. If a person is highly motivated when reading one text, thus inflating the scores for that condition, he/she will also tend to be well motivated when reading other texts and so will inflate those scores as well. The point about using a same-subjects design is that any individual peculiarities get equalized out over all conditions. In fact, each person acts as their own control.

This is known as a **within-subjects** or **related design**, because the comparison is *within* the same group of subjects, the scores from each subject being related. Another term which is sometimes used to describe a related design is **repeated measures**. This is because the scores which measure performance are repeatedly taken from the same subjects.

The main disadvantage of the same subjects doing all conditions is the exact opposite of different-subjects designs. Because everyone is doing all experimental conditions they are likely to be influenced by other experimental conditions. For example, if the subjects do all the conditions in the same order, what effect may earlier conditions have on the performance of later conditions? Suppose a researcher designed an experiment in which subjects have to learn two lists of words, list A being long words and list B short words. Suppose everyone learned list A before list B. Some subjects might learn from the first list how to tackle the second list. Other subjects might be fatigued by the time they get to the end of list B. These are called **order effects** because they depend on the *order* in which conditions are done. The worry from the experimenter's point of view is that order effects are irrelevant to the predicted difference between learning long words and short words.

It is for this reason that it is normal practice for researchers to vary the order of conditions so that half the subjects learn list A first and list B second and the other half list B first and list A second. The idea is that any practice or boredom effects will be equalized out because list A will be first on half the occasions and list B first on the other half. This results in **counterbalanced orders** between the two conditions.

There may also be occasions when subjects have to be given different experimental materials so that they do not become too familiar with them. If there were two lists of words to be learnt under different conditions, two versions of the word lists would have to be prepared. Otherwise, the subjects who read the same list twice would have partially learned it in the first condition. The two lists would have to be *counterbalanced* so that each list was read first or second.

All this goes to show is how many things have to be taken into account when designing an experiment. The point is to try and eliminate all possible irrelevant variables which might be affecting subjects' performance (the selection of word lists, the order of presentation, and so on). The only difference between the two conditions should be the predicted differences in recall for different lists of words.

The dilemma is that, if the experimenter decides to use the *same* subjects, then the experimental materials have to be carefully matched and presented in a counterbalanced order. If the experimenter uses *different* subjects, the same lists can be used for the two conditions because each subject only learns one list. But the problem is that the two groups of subjects may vary in ways which are irrelevant to the purpose of the experiment.

▶ **Progress box two**

Same or different subjects

	Advantages	*Disadvantages*
Between-subjects (unrelated design)	• Necessary for natural groups, e.g. different levels of ability, age or gender • Necessary for experiments in which subjects are misled or taken by surprise • No order effects	• Individual differences may affect performance (partially offset by matching subjects or allocating them randomly to groups)
Within-subjects (related design)	• Eliminates individual differences because each subject produces scores in all experimental conditions (repeated measures)	• Cannot be used when subjects *have* to be different, e.g. men and women • Problems of counterbalancing order effects, experimental materials, etc.

3 Introduction to statistical analysis

3.1 Variability of scores

We now come back to the problem that, however much you try to eliminate irrelevant variables in your experimental design, you can never get rid of *all* the variability in people's behaviour. This variability in subjects' performance will inevitably be reflected in whatever measure you take of the dependent variable. So what you will find yourself faced with is experimental data consisting of a whole range of different scores by subjects. What you want to know is: are the differences in the scores the result of manipulating the independent variable? Or are there no real differences apart from unpredictable fluctuations in people's performance due to random variables, as stated by the null hypothesis?

Suppose the experimental hypothesis is that people will have better memory recall for simple texts than for complex texts. The independent variable is tested by giving one group of subjects a simple text to read and another group a complex text. Numbers of ideas recalled is the measure of the dependent variable. When you run the experiment with a number of subjects you will end up with a set of individual recall scores for the subjects in each condition.

If the subjects had all reacted in exactly the same way, so that they *all* got better recall scores for simple texts, you might feel pretty confident about saying that the experimental hypothesis had been supported. But, of course, people are not all the same. Their performance on a memory recall task will vary for all sorts of reasons that have nothing to do with the experimental prediction about simple and complex texts.

Imagine that, after running the experiment, you end up with recall scores for ten subjects in each condition as shown in Table 3.1. These recall scores represent the number of ideas recalled by each subject. The first thing to do is to calculate the *average* recall scores for the two conditions (this average is known as the **mean** for each condition). To

Table 3.1   Number of ideas recalled (out of 10)

	Condition 1 (simple texts)	Condition 2 (complex texts)
	10	2
	5	1
	6	3
	3	4
	9	4
	8	4
	7	2
	5	5
	6	7
	5	4
Totals	64	36
Means	6.4	3.6

calculate the mean for condition 1 add up the total number of ideas for all ten subjects, which is 64. Divide this total by 10 (the number of subjects in condition 1) to get the mean for condition 1 of 6.4. Do the same for the condition 2 scores. Remember that it is always essential to calculate the means for each condition.

The next step is to work out the *difference* between the means for condition 1 and condition 2, which is 6.4 − 3.6 = 2.8. The question we now have to ask is whether this difference between the means is large enough to represent a *real* difference between condition 1 and condition 2 when we take into account all the variability in scores. There would be no problem if each and every subject in condition 1 had recalled exactly 6.4 ideas while every one in condition 2 had recalled 3.6 ideas. In that case it would be reasonable to claim that the subjects in condition 1 scored more highly than those in condition 2. But life is not that easy. The mean for condition 1 represents a numerical average around which there is quite a wide range of scores, from as little as 3 to as many as 10 out of 10.

What is the range of scores in condition 2?

As you can see from Table 3.1, scores in condition 2 range from 1 to 7 ideas recalled. In other words, there is a considerable amount of variability in scores around the means for subjects who are doing exactly the same experimental condition.

The best way to look at total variability is to plot all the subjects' recall scores in a **histogram** like that shown in Figure 3.1. The histogram shows number of ideas recalled along the bottom, i.e. all possible scores

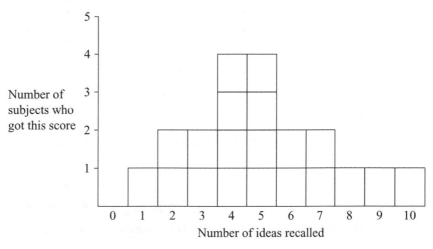

Figure 3.1 Plotting a histogram

from 0 to 10 ideas. We have used all 20 subjects from both conditions. For each subject, there is a *square* which represents their particular recall score, which you should check against Table 3.1.

? Question 4 (a) How many subjects recalled 5 ideas?

(b) Did more subjects recall 4 or 7 ideas?

(c) Did any subject recall no ideas?

(d) Did any subject recall all 10 ideas?

(e) How many subjects were there altogether?

It is obvious from the histogram in Figure 3.1 that there is quite a lot of variability in the number of correct ideas recalled. Clearly *means* do not tell us everything we need to know about subjects' scores. We also need a measure of the variability of scores around the mean. The histogram in Figure 3.1 shows the *total variability* in all the subjects' scores. But what we are really interested in is the *differences* between the recall scores of the subjects in the two different experimental conditions. In Figure 3.2 the two sets of scores are presented as separate histograms. Check that these histograms represent the same recall scores as those shown for condition 1 and condition 2 in Table 3.1. There should be ten squares for the ten subjects in each condition.

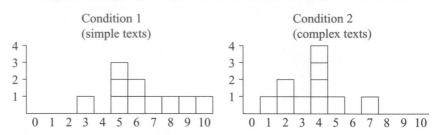

Figure 3.2   Histograms for condition 1 and condition 2

? Question 5   (a) How many subjects in condition 1 recalled 5 ideas?

(b) How many subjects in condition 2 recalled 5 ideas?

(c) Did the condition 1 or the condition 2 subjects recall more ideas?

(d) How many subjects in condition 2 had a higher recall score than at least one person in condition 1?

The histograms in Figure 3.2 demonstrate two points. You will remember that there is a relatively large difference between the *means* of the two conditions, 6.4 ideas correct for condition 1 as against 3.6 ideas correct for condition 2, as shown in Table 3.1. On the other hand, there is quite a lot of variability of scores around the means in both conditions. You will notice that the variability is greater in condition 1, with the scores spread out from 3 to 10, while the scores in condition 2 are more bunched together.

The difference between the means in the predicted direction that condition 1 (simple texts) will produce higher scores appears to support the experimental hypothesis. But when we look at the variability in scores things are not so clear-cut. What about the subject in condition 1 who got only 3 ideas correct or the subject in condition 2 who managed to get 7 out of 10 ideas correct? These scores appear to go against the experimental hypothesis that more ideas will be recalled from simple texts.

How can a researcher decide whether any differences in scores are due to the manipulation of an independent variable, as predicted by the experimental hypothesis, or whether the differences are due to random performance, as stated by the null hypothesis? This is a real problem for psychologists because most of the information from psychological experiments is of this kind: differences in means between conditions, combined with a lot of variability in individual subjects' scores.

The whole point about statistical tests is that they can settle this question for you. Do the results from your experiment represent a significant difference in favour of the experimental hypothesis? If so, you are entitled to reject the null hypothesis that there are only random differences due to unpredictable variables.

3.2 Statistical probabilities

With all the variability in subjects' scores, it would be rare indeed to find absolutely clear-cut differences between the scores for different experimental conditions. So all a statistical test can provide is a probability that your results are significant. The way this is done may seem rather paradoxical. Statistical tests refer to probabilities that any differences in scores *are* due to random variability caused by unpredictable variables. This means that the *less* probable it is that any differences are due to random variability, the *more* confident you can be that there is a real significant difference due to your manipulation of the independent variable.

This is the basis of all **statistical tests of significance**. Statistical tests tell you the probability of getting the differences in scores found in your experiment if scores are in fact occurring on a random basis. If this probability is very low, then you can reject the null hypothesis that the differences are random. Instead you can accept the experimental hypothesis that your experimental results are significant, i.e. that they are *not* likely to be random.

Statistical tables provide a *distribution* of all the probabilities of experimental scores occurring randomly. This makes it possible to look up the percentage probability of the results being due to random variability. On this basis you can decide whether a very small percentage probability (say, only 1 per cent) that your results are random is low enough to entitle you to reject the null hypothesis, and accept your results as a *significant* difference in favour of the experimental hypothesis.

One important point we should emphasize here is that when we are talking about whether an experimental result is significant, there is always a specific percentage probability that *every* experimental result is a random result. To get this idea across, suppose you tossed a coin a thousand times and got heads every time. You would probably think that the coin was definitely biased towards heads. However, there is a tiny probability that a run of a thousand heads in a row could occur even with an unbiased coin. However, because the probability of this happening is so small, you would be likely to accept that the coin *is* biased.

It is just the same with experimental results. A big difference in mean scores between conditions is probably due to the predicted effects of the independent variable rather than random variability. But there is always a small probability that the differences are due to random variability. So there can never be a 100 per cent certainty that the scores in an experiment are due to the effects of manipulating the independent variable. The most you can say is that the probability of the results being due to random variability is so tiny that it is permissible to reject the null hypothesis and accept instead that there is a significant difference between the experimental conditions as predicted by the experimental hypothesis.

3.3   Selecting a level of significance

So far we have not really tackled the question of why a researcher would be prepared to accept a particular percentage probability of a random result when deciding whether or not to reject the null hypothesis. What risk would be acceptable that the scores resulting from the experiment occurred randomly, as stated by the null hypothesis, and were not significant at all? Of course, you would like to be 100 per cent certain that the difference in scores is significant. But, as we said earlier, you can never be 100 per cent certain that it is not a freak random occurrence. Would you accept a 99 per cent probability that your result is significant against a 1 per cent probability that it is random (i.e. a 1 in 100 chance that it is a random result)? Or would you accept a 95 per cent probability of significance against a 5 per cent probability that it is random (i.e. a 1 in 20 probability that it is a random result)?

These percentage probabilities are known as **levels of significance**. There is no simple answer as to what level of significance is acceptable. It is up to experimenters to decide what odds they are prepared to accept when deciding whether the results of an experiment are significant. For this reason, experimenters always have to state the probability of a random result which is being used to accept or reject the null hypothesis.

Imagine that you are investigating whether a new reading scheme might help backward children and you carried out an experiment in which you compared the progress of a group of children using your new scheme against a control group using traditional methods. Suppose you found a difference in reading improvement scores between the two groups in favour of the new scheme. Suppose the probability that this difference could have occurred randomly was 5 per cent (i.e. a 1 in 20 probability that there were only random differences rather than a significant difference caused by the reading scheme). Would you accept that the difference was significant and introduce the new reading scheme, and at what cost in materials and teacher training? Imagine another case where you are testing a powerful drug with nasty side-effects and find an improvement in patients taking the drug as compared with a control group. If the difference between the groups could have occurred by chance 5 in 100 times, would you accept that the difference is significant and introduce the new drug? Would you change your odds if you knew that without the drug most of the patients would die anyway? And how would you feel if an aeroplane you were going to fly in had a 5 per cent probability of developing electrical failure?

These examples bring home the fact that choosing a significance level is always a matter of deciding what odds you are prepared to accept that your results are due to chance. In the case of the reading scheme no one would probably suffer all that much if it was due to random variability after all; as long as it was not too expensive, you would probably go ahead and introduce the new scheme.

On the other hand, you might feel more doubtful about introducing a powerful drug with side-effects if there was a 1 in 20 probability that it was doing no good at all; although you might accept these odds if it were the only hope of saving people's lives. I don't think any of us would fly in a plane with a 1 in 20 chance of crashing.

In psychology (possibly because it is thought that nothing too terrible can happen as a result of accepting a result as significant!) it is a convention to accept odds of either 1 per cent or 5 per cent as grounds for rejecting the null hypothesis and instead accepting that the experimental hypothesis has been supported. The way this is expressed is to state that the probability of a result being due to chance is less than 1 per cent or less than 5 per cent. That is why in articles in psychological journals you will see statements that differences between experimental conditions are significant ($p < 0.01$) or ($p < 0.05$). This means that the probability (p) of a result occurring by chance is less than (expressed as $<$) 1 per cent (0.01) or 5 per cent (0.05). Sometimes, you will find other probabilities quoted such as $p < 0.02$ or $p < 0.001$. These represent probabilities of obtaining a chance result of 2 times in 100 and 1 in 1000 (2 per cent and 0.1 per cent). Clearly these give you even greater grounds for rejecting the null hypothesis that your results are due to the effects of random variability.

? Question 6 Suppose that an experimenter reports that a significant difference has been found between subjects' recall scores for simple and complex texts ($p < 0.001$).

(a) Which of the following represents the smallest probability of a random result? The null hypothesis can be rejected because the probability of the difference being due to random variability is less than:

1 in 100 (1 per cent)   1 in 20 (5 per cent)   1 in 1000 (0.1 per cent)

(b) Which of the above significance levels would indicate the greatest level of significance?

Statistical textbooks propose that researchers should first select a significance level, for instance, $p < 0.05$. They would have to stick with this significance level, so all they can claim is that their results are significant ($p < 0.05$). It often happens that results may be much more significant than this, say $p < 0.001$, but strictly they should only be quoted at the originally selected significance level of $p < 0.05$. However, psychologists are normal human beings. If they find that their results are significant at the 1 per cent level ($p < 0.01$) they will say so.

Statistical tables provide lists of percentage probabilities of random variability. To use these tables the first thing you will have to do is calculate the value of an appropriate 'statistic' from your own scores. The step-by-step procedures for the statistical tests will tell you how to do this. You will also be instructed how to look up the value of the 'statistic' in the appropriate statistical tables to find out whether it is significant and, if so, at what significance level.

 Progress box three

Statistical significance

- Subjects' scores in different experimental conditions vary around the *mean*.
- *Variability in scores* will be due both to independent variables manipulated by the experimenter and to random variables which are irrelevant to the experimental hypothesis.
- *Statistical tests* give percentage probabilities that the scores from an experiment are due to random variables, as stated by the null hypothesis.
- If a *percentage probability* is below a certain level, normally 1 per cent ($p < 0.01$) or 5 per cent ($p < 0.05$), the experimenter can reject the null hypothesis and accept instead support for the experimental hypothesis that there are significant differences.

3.4   One-tailed and two-tailed hypotheses

There is one further point about the way an experimental hypothesis is formulated which has implications for the way in which you look up probabilities in statistical tables. This is whether the experimental hypothesis is *one-tailed* or *two-tailed*.

A **one-tailed hypothesis** is one that, as its name implies, makes a prediction in one particular direction. An example might be that short sentences will result in more ideas being remembered than long sentences. But there are other hypotheses which make a prediction by predicting that the effect of an independent variable may go in either direction. In our example, this would mean predicting that short sentences will result in either more ideas being remembered or fewer ideas being remembered, i.e. predicting that sentence length will have some effect but not being prepared to say what. This is called a **two-tailed hypothesis** because it predicts differences in two directions, indicating that a difference in either direction will be acceptable.

It is obviously preferable to be able to give an explanation of human behaviour in terms of predicting behaviour in one direction rather than to make the more vague prediction that there will be an effect of some kind in either direction. However, there are times, particularly during the more exploratory phase of a research programme, when you might just want to try out whether a variable has an effect, for example, whether a teaching method has any effect, good or bad, on children learning to read.

One-tailed and two-tailed hypotheses have implications for statistical analysis. The point is that for a hypothesis which predicts a difference in only *one* direction, there is a specific percentage probability that the difference might occur randomly. But, if a hypothesis makes a prediction that a difference might occur in *either* direction, then there is *double* the probability that such differences might occur randomly. There is the probability that a random difference might occur in one direction plus the probability of a random difference in the other direction. This in effect doubles the probability that the differences in scores may be due to random variability

Imagine that the probability of a random result in one direction is 1 per cent. This means that you can reject the null hypothesis at the $p < 0.01$ level of significance. But suppose your original prediction had been two-tailed in either direction. Then there would be double the probability that it was a random result, i.e. 2 per cent. You would not be able to reject the null hypothesis at the 1 per cent ($p < 0.01$) level but only at the 2 per cent ($p < 0.02$) level. In other words, with a two-tailed hypothesis there is a higher probability that it is a random result.

Some statistical tables give either one-tailed or two-tailed probabilities, not always both. Sometimes you will have to double the one-tailed probabilities for a two-tailed test, or halve the two-tailed probabilities for a one-tailed test, in order to arrive at the correct level of significance. You will be given detailed instructions about what to do for each test.

3.5   Looking up probabilities in statistical tables

The purpose of **statistical tables** is to test whether predicted differences reach a certain level of significance (e.g. 1 per cent or 5 per cent).

The first step is to calculate a **statistic** based on the scores in your experiment. You will be given full instructions about how to calculate these for each statistical test. It is this statistic that you will be looking up in the appropriate statistical table.

When looking up the statistic in statistical tables, you will have to take into account the total number of subjects in your experiment and/or the number of subjects in each experimental condition. This is because the probabilities of getting a big difference between conditions depends on how large a sample of subjects you have tested. Furthermore, for some tests you will find that you have to look up one statistical table for small numbers of subjects and another table when you have used more subjects. Sometimes the number of experimental conditions in your experiment is also relevant for looking up probabilities in a statistical table. Remember, too, that whether your experimental hypothesis is one-tailed or two-tailed affects the significance level of the probabilities.

But do not worry, you will be given full instructions about how to look up the probabilities in each statistical table.

4 Selecting a statistical test

Basic principles for selecting tests

Now we come to the all-important chapter as far as your ability to use statistical tests is concerned. And you should be encouraged to note that this is one of the shortest chapters in the book. The vital consideration is to choose an appropriate statistical test for each type of experimental design. The whole art of using statistics is to match up the experimental designs described in Chapter 2 with the statistical tests listed in the remaining chapters of this book.

The reason for this is that the calculation of percentage probabilities of obtaining a random result is based on the amount of variability in subjects' scores. The point was made in Chapter 2 that certain decisions about experimental designs, like deciding whether to use same or different subjects, will affect the variability in subjects' scores. Since each statistical test is based on a particular distribution of percentage probabilities, different statistical tests will be appropriate for experimental designs which produce different amounts of random variability.

So the first and most important point we want to emphasize is this: *the selection of an appropriate statistical test follows from the experimental design you have chosen to test your experimental hypothesis.* In fact, choice of a suitable test depends on *very few* decisions about experimental design. Once you have made these decisions you will find that you have automatically selected which statistical test to use for analysing the significance of your experimental data. These decisions are summarized in the following sections.

Same versus different subjects

One of the most important criteria for selecting a statistical test depends on whether the same subjects have been used for all conditions or whether different subjects have been used.

Reread Chapter 2, Sections 2.3 and 2.4, and Progress box two to refresh your memory about the advantages and disadvantages of using same and different subjects.

You will remember that there are several equivalent names for same-subjects and different-subjects experimental designs, as shown below.

Equivalent experimental designs

Same subjects	Different subjects
Within-subjects	Between-subjects
Related designs	Unrelated designs
Repeated measures	

The most usual terms are **related designs** versus **unrelated designs**. These terms sum up the crucial distinctions between the two types of design. Scores taken from the same subjects in experimental conditions are related because they come from the same subject, which is why they are called *related designs*. Scores taken from different subjects doing each experimental condition are different for each subject, which is why they are known as *unrelated designs*. You will find that decisions about appropriate statistical tests depends on whether a test is designed for *related* or *unrelated* designs.

4.3   Number of experimental conditions

Another relevant consideration is how many experimental conditions there are in an experiment.

Reread Chapter 2, Sections 2.1 and 2.2, to refresh your memory about the rationale for selecting two or more experimental and control conditions.

Some statistical tests are designed to analyse experiments with only *two* conditions, in which the experimental hypothesis predicts differences between two conditions. Experimental designs with *three or more conditions* involve more complex statistical comparisons between sets of scores. Other statistical tests can analyse whether there is a *trend* in scores from smallest to largest scores over three conditions or more. Trend tests should be used when the experimental hypothesis predicts a specific order of conditions.

4.4   Using the decision charts

There are two main categories of statistical tests introduced in this book. These are called non-parametric tests and parametric tests.

In Part II you will be introduced to **non-parametric tests**. These tests are suitable for the kinds of experimental designs described in Chapter 2. The characteristic feature of these designs is that only *one independent variable* is tested in each experiment.

Parametric tests can handle experimental designs in which more than one independent variable can be varied at the same time. These more sophisticated experimental designs and the more complex statistical calculations will not be introduced until Part III. So all you need to worry about for the time being are the non-parametric tests in Part II.

Because of the differences between non-parametric and parametric tests, there are two decision charts. Decision Chart 1 is to be found inside the *front cover* of the book; it only deals with the selection of non-parametric tests. Decision Chart 2, which is to be found inside the *back cover*, is a complete chart which covers *all* the tests described in the book. For the non-parametric tests in Part II you will only need to use Decision Chart 1. It is not until Part III that it will be necessary to consult Decision Chart 2. Full instructions will be given for using each of the decision charts.

The way to use **Decision Chart 1** is to look at the diamond boxes. Each of these asks a question to which an answer has to be given. You need to follow a path through the chart depending on your answers. Eventually you will be directed to a square box which contains the appropriate statistical tests to be selected for a particular research design.

The experimental designs described in Chapter 2 were concerned with predicted *differences* between experimental conditions. For these designs you should start with the diamond box at the top of the chart in the centre, asking whether an experiment is investigating 'Differences between conditions?' The answer should be 'yes' and you then need to answer the questions about 'How many experimental conditions?' and 'Same or different subjects?' This will lead you to one of the statistical tests which will be described in Chapters 6 and 7.

 Progress box four

All you need to know about statistics

Before the experiment

- Formulate your *experimental hypothesis* in terms of the predicted effects you expect to occur as a result of manipulating independent variables.
- By implication, the *null hypothesis* is that the results of your experiment will be due not to the effects predicted by the experimental hypothesis, but to random variables which are unknown and unpredictable.
- Use the decision charts to decide which is the appropriate *statistical test* for comparing your experimental results against the probability that they occurred randomly.

After the experiment

- Carry out the appropriate calculations on your experimental scores to calculate a 'statistic'.
- Look up this statistic in the appropriate statistical table (taking into account whether your experimental hypothesis is one-tailed or two-tailed) to see whether the probability of your result being random is less than 5 per cent ($p < 0.05$) or 1 per cent ($p < 0.01$).
- Decide whether you have to accept the null hypothesis that your results are due to random variability, or whether you can reject the null hypothesis and interpret your results as supporting the experimental hypothesis.

Part II   Non-parametric tests

5 General method for non-parametric tests

5.1 Preparing the data

It is essential to make it clear whether the scores from an experiment came from the same subjects doing all experimental conditions or different groups of subjects doing each condition. There is a convention about how to indicate this in the tables for showing scores. For related designs using the *same subjects* in all conditions, the convention is to list subjects in the left-hand column, numbering them from 1 upwards. In Table 5.1 it is clear that each of the four subjects did both conditions, producing pairs of scores, one in condition 1 and one in condition 2. For instance, subject 1 obtained a pair of scores, a score of 10 for condition 1 and a score of 5 for condition 2. These pairs of scores can be thought of as *related* because they both come from the same subject.

When *different subjects* do each condition there will be no subjects column. The scores for each condition will be listed as in Table 5.2. In this case each score comes from a different subject. Because of this the scores from *different* subjects can be thought of as *unrelated*.

Before we start any statistical calculations, it is essential to calculate the *means* of the scores for each experimental condition. The means demonstrate whether the difference between conditions is in the predicted direction. It is necessary to select a statistical test to check that

Table 5.1 Scores of same subjects (related design)

Subjects	Condition 1	Condition 2
1	10	5
2	15	10
3	25	5
4	10	10

Table 5.2   Scores of different subjects (unrelated design)

Condition 1	Condition 2
10	5
15	10
25	5
10	10

any difference is significant. But there is no point in doing this if there are no differences in the means or they go in the wrong direction.

? Question 7   (a) Calculate the means for condition 1 and condition 2 in Table 5.1 and Table 5.2.

(b) Are there any differences between the scores in Table 5.1 and Table 5.2?

5.2   Assigning ranks to scores

For non-parametric tests comparisons of subjects' performance are made on the basis of whether scores are higher or lower in different experimental conditions. In order to establish which scores are higher or lower it is necessary to **rank** scores in terms of their relative size. To rank scores all you have to do is assign ranks of 1, 2, 3, 4, etc. to each score in order of their magnitude, starting with the smallest score, as in Table 5.3.

You will notice that we have assigned rank 1 to the smallest score of 3.

Table 5.3   Ranking scores

Scores	Ranks
6	4
3	1
12	7
4	2
7	5
5	3
8	6

This starting point is arbitrary. Provided that you observe the order of magnitude of the scores, there is nothing to stop you giving rank 1 to the biggest score, 2 to the next biggest, ending up by giving the highest rank to the smallest score. But we shall always stick to *smallest* first, as in Table 5.3, giving rank 1 to the smallest score of 3, rank 2 to the next smallest score of 4, and so on, ending with the highest rank of 7 for the biggest score of 12.

Sometimes a subject may produce a *zero score*, for example, someone may not remember a single word from a text and so score 'zero' words. As far as ranks are concerned, a zero would count as the lowest possible score and so be assigned rank 1.

5.3 Dealing with tied scores

Ties occur when some of the scores to be ranked are the same. Look at the scores in Table 5.4. Three subjects produced scores of 1 and there are also two scores of 4. What rank should we give to the three scores of 1? Should these scores all be given rank 1 because they are the smallest scores? But then, what rank should be given to the next biggest score of 2?

The procedure is to assign to the **tied scores** the *average* of the ranks they would have been entitled to. The three tied scores of 1 in Table 5.4 would have been assigned ranks 1, 2 and 3 because these are the lowest ranks. So all three tied scores are given the average of these ranks: $1 + 2 + 3 = 6$, and $6 \div 3 = 2$. This results in the three tied scores of 1 each being assigned the average rank of 2.

The next smallest score is 2. Since the ranks of 1, 2 and 3 have already been used up, this score is assigned the next available rank of 4. The next score of 3 is assigned rank 5. But what about the two tied scores of 4?

Table 5.4 Ranking tied scores

Scores	Ranks
1	2
2	4
1	2
4	6.5
1	2
3	5
4	6.5
6	9
5	8

These would be entitled to the ranks of 6 and 7. Since the average of 6 and 7 is 6.5 the tied scores of 4 are both assigned ranks of 6.5. The next score of 5 will be assigned the next available rank of 8 and the biggest score of 6 gets the highest rank of 9.

One good tip for checking up whether you have assigned tied ranks correctly is to check whether the number of ranks is the same as the numbers of scores, e.g. in Table 5.4 there are 9 scores and the highest rank is 9.

? Question 8   Assign ranks to the scores in Table 5.5.

Table 5.5   Assigning ranks

Scores	Ranks
4	
8	
3	
3	
1	
7	
4	

5.4   Rank ordering of unrelated scores

So far we have been looking at a single set of scores in order to introduce the principle of how to rank scores and how to deal with ties. In *unrelated designs* the scores come from different subjects performing under different experimental conditions, as shown in Table 5.6.

Table 5.6   Overall ranking of unrelated scores

Condition 1		Condition 2	
Scores	Ranks	Scores	Ranks
1	1	2	2.5
4	5	6	7
5	6	3	4
2	2.5	7	8

All the scores are unrelated and so have to be ranked as if they were one overall set of ranks. The lowest score in either condition is the score of 1 in condition 1. The next lowest scores are 2 in condition 1 and 2 in condition 2. Because these are tied scores they are assigned the appropriate average ranks of 2 and 3, i.e. 2.5. The rest of the ranks are assigned in the usual way, ending with a rank of 8 for the highest score of 7. The important point to notice is that the ranks apply *across both conditions* because the scores are ranked as an overall set of unrelated scores.

? **Question 9**   Assign ranks to the *unrelated* scores in Table 5.7.

Table 5.7   Assigning ranks to unrelated scores

Condition 1		Condition 2	
Scores	*Ranks*	*Scores*	*Ranks*
1		3	
4		4	
6		5	
2		7	

5.5   Rank ordering of related scores

When we are dealing with *related designs* using the same subjects in both experimental conditions, it is possible to make a direct comparison between each subject's pairs of scores under both experimental conditions. The way to do this is to calculate the *differences* between each subject's scores for condition 1 and condition 2, as shown in Table 5.8. (Note that it is arbitrary whether you subtract condition 1 from condition 2 or the other way round.) It is a convention, however, always to subtract condition 2 from condition 1 when calculating differences in scores. Ranks are then assigned to these differences between scores in just the same way as ranks are assigned to scores (see column for Ranks in Table 5.8).

You will notice in Table 5.8 that we applied exactly the same procedure for assigning average ranks to *tied differences*. Thus an average rank of 2 was given to the three tied differences of 1 and average ranks of 6.5 were given to the two tied differences of 4. But what about the difference of 0 produced by subject 8? Why didn't we assign a rank to

Table 5.8   Ranking differences between pairs of related scores

Subject	Condition 1	Condition 2	Differences	Ranks
1	6	5	1	2
2	7	5	2	4
3	3	2	1	2
4	5	1	4	6.5
5	5	4	1	2
6	5	2	3	5
7	5	1	4	6.5
8	4	4	0	(tie)
9	7	1	6	9
10	6	1	5	8

this difference just as we would have done for a zero score? The point is that subject 8 produced the *same* score of 4 for both condition 1 and for condition 2. So this subject's scores do not represent a difference in favour of either experimental condition. Since this is truly a *nil* difference as far as the comparison between conditions is concerned, tied scores *across conditions* are given a difference score of zero. This kind of tie is dropped altogether from the analysis of differences in scores in favour of condition 1 or condition 2, shown by the (tie) in the Ranks column for subject 8.

5.6   Ranking positive and negative scores

So far we have considered only positive differences between scores but sometimes you will find negative differences, as in Table 5.9. What you do in a case like this is to *ignore* the plus and minus signs when ranking the differences. This is because you need to calculate how many of the differences are in favour of one condition or the other. Pluses mean that scores in condition 1 are higher than in condition 2. Minuses mean that scores in condition 2 are higher than in condition 1.

In order to calculate these small or large plus or minus differences you need to rank all the differences together, *regardless of whether they are plus or minus*. In Table 5.9 the average rank of 1.5 is allocated to the smallest scores of 1 (+1, −1) and an average rank of 4 to the three next smallest scores of 2 (−2, +2, −2) and so on, thus ending up with a single set of ranks for the differences in the Ranks column not counting ties.

Table 5.9   Ranking positive and minus scores

Subjects	Condition 1	Condition 2	Differences	Ranks
1	3	5	−2	4
2	5	3	+2	4
3	3	2	+1	1.5
4	0	5	−5	7.5
5	4	4	0	(tie)
6	2	5	−3	6
7	3	5	−2	4
8	0	0	0	(tie)
9	6	1	+5	7.5
10	4	5	−1	1.5

? Question 10 Look at the Ranks column in Table 5.9.

(a) Why is the 0 score for subject 4 not given a (tie) in the Ranks column?

(b) Why is the 0 for subjects 5 and 8 counted as a tie?

(c) Why is the highest rank 7.5 when there are eight scores (not counting the two ties for equal scores for subjects 5 and 8)?

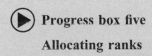

Progress box five

Allocating ranks

Overall ranking of unrelated scores

- Assign ranks across both conditions.
- Assign the lowest rank of 1 to the lowest score, the next rank of 2 to the next lowest score, and so on.
- Zero scores are counted as being the lowest possible score and are therefore assigned the lowest ranks.
- When there are tied scores these are assigned the *average* of the ranks which should have been given to these scores.

> **Ranking of differences between pairs of related scores**
>
> • Calculate the differences between each pair of scores (condition 1 minus condition 2).
> • Ranks are assigned to differences between pairs of scores in the same way as to actual scores, with the lowest rank being assigned to the lowest difference, and so on.
> • When there are no differences between *pairs of scores*, indicating no difference in favour of either condition, this difference is allocated a (tie) in the Ranks column.
> • Ties *between differences* are allocated ranks based on the average of the ranks which should have been allocated to these differences.
> • Positive and minus differences are ranked together as a single series of ranks, *ignoring* the plus and minus signs.

5.7 Calculating rank totals

Having worked out the rank scores, the next issue is how can they be used to estimate the ranks for each experimental condition? The way this is done is to calculate the **rank totals** for each condition. Look back at the ranks in Table 5.6. You will remember that these scores were from different subjects in an unrelated design. In order to test whether there is a significant difference between condition 1 and condition 2 we need to calculate the totals of ranks for each condition. If you add up the total of ranks for condition 1, you get 14.5. The total for condition 2 comes to 21.5. Because the lowest ranks are assigned to the smallest scores, this indicates that the ranked scores in condition 2 are higher than those in condition 1.

? Question 11 Look at Table 5.10.

(a) Calculate the means of the scores for each condition.

(b) Calculate the rank totals for each condition.

(c) Do the means and the rank totals reflect the same differences between conditions?

Table 5.10 Calculating means and rank totals

	Condition 1		Condition 2	
	Scores	*Ranks*	*Scores*	*Ranks*
	1	1	3	3
	4	4.5	4	4.5
	6	7	5	6
	2	2	7	8
Rank totals				
Means				

Table 5.8 showed the ranks of differences between pairs of scores from each subject in a related design. These ranked differences add up to 45. The tie for subject 8 is omitted from the calculation of the ranked differences total because this subject showed no difference in favour of either condition. Remember, too, that it doesn't matter at this stage whether the differences are minus or plus; you simply add up the total of all ranks, both plus and minus. When it comes to the statistical calculations it will become necessary to separate out the differences going in one direction (minus) from those going in the other direction (plus).

Question 12 Look at Table 5.9.

(a) Calculate the means for each condition.

(b) Add up the ranked differences in the Ranks column.

5.8 Looking up non-parametric statistical tables

The aim is to test whether the differences in rank totals for two or more experimental conditions are sufficiently different to indicate a significant difference between the experimental conditions in the predicted direction. For each set of scores a **statistic** is calculated which reflects the differences between rank totals. It is the value of this statistic which is looked up in the appropriate statistical table. If the statistic reaches an acceptable significance level, this indicates that the differences in rank totals between conditions are larger than would be expected randomly. In this case the null hypothesis that there are random differences can be rejected and the experimental hypothesis supported.

One point that you are bound to notice is that the statistical tables for non-parametric tests all look quite different. All the tables provide exactly the same information about the probabilities of a statistic based on rank totals being significant. However, sometimes the significance levels are along the top of the table and you have to check the probability values for each significance level. In other tables the number of conditions or subjects are set out along the top and the probabilities are given in the table itself. Sometimes the statistic you have calculated has to be larger than the probability values in the table and sometimes smaller. Sometimes the values are given for one-tailed tests and sometimes for two-tailed tests.

All this may seem a recipe for disaster, but the reason is simply that each of the statisticians who gave their name to a test calculated their own tables in the format that they had selected for themselves. But do not be alarmed. You will be given precise instructions about how to look up the significance levels in a statistical table for each test.

5.9   Non-parametric tests, step by step

We will be presenting non-parametric tests in the order shown in Table 5.11. Tests for *two conditions* are described in Chapter 6 and tests for *three or more conditions* and *trends* in Chapter 7. Two other types of non-parametric tests for correlations and the chi-square test will be introduced in Chapters 8 and 9. Full details will be given in these chapters so you won't have to worry about them until then.

Table 5.11   Non-parametric tests

	Related designs (same subjects)	*Unrelated designs (different subjects)*
Chapter 6 Two conditions	Wilcoxon	Mann–Whitney
Chapter 7 Three or more conditions	Friedman Page's L trend	Kruskal–Wallis Jonckheere trend
Chapter 8	Correlations	
Chapter 9	Chi-square	

The detailed description of each of the tests presented in the following chapters is divided into seven sections.

1 *When to use.* In this section you are reminded of the experimental designs for which you can use the test.

2 *Sample data.* This gives a sample set of data which can be analysed using the test.

3 *Hypothesis.* This states the prediction that the experiment is designed to test.

4 *Rationale.* Under this heading the aims of the test are explained and information is provided to help you understand the reasons for doing the required calculations. It may be helpful to read this through rather quickly before doing the test and then go back to it afterwards.

5 *Step-by-step instructions.* This section goes through a worked example using the sample data with a clear statement of all the steps and calculations you need to carry out when doing the test.

6 *Looking up significance in tables.* This section helps you to find your way around statistical tables and decide whether the data in your experiment are significant.

7 *Conclusions.* This section states the results of the experiment and whether they are significant at a specific level of significance.

Note about calculations

We have done all the calculations for these statistical tests with an ordinary pocket calculator. The final answers have been rounded off to a number of decimal places. If you do the calculations by hand, and/or round figures up or down as you go along, you may find that your answers differ from ours in the last decimal place – nothing to worry about, of course.

Note about names of tests

Sometimes you may have to recall the *names* of statistical tests from memory. All the tests have been invented by different statisticians who thought up each test and calculated the probabilities in the statistical tables. It just so happens that the related tests for experiments using same subjects were each invented by just *one* statistician, i.e. Wilcoxon, Friedman and Page. In contrast, the unrelated tests for experiments using different subjects were invented by pairs of statisticians and so are named after both, with a dash between them, i.e. Mann–Whitney, Kruskal–Wallis. Jonckheere is the only exception because he invented his own unrelated trend test. I hope this will be a useful tip for remembering the appropriate related or unrelated tests.

6 Non-parametric tests (two conditions)

6.1 Wilcoxon test (related)

When to use

The Wilcoxon test should be used for a *related design* when the same subjects are used in *two conditions*.

Sample data

A researcher was interested in whether people find it easier to learn a list of words while listening to music (condition 2) or without music (condition 1). All subjects learned one list with music and one list without music. To control for order effects, half the subjects learnt first with music and then without music while the other half of the subjects did the conditions in the reverse order. Recall scores are shown in Table 6.1.

Hypothesis

The experimenter predicted that students would be more relaxed when listening to music and so would recall more words in the music condition.

? Question 13 Is this a one-tailed or a two-tailed hypothesis?

Table 6.1 Recall scores for lists presented with and without music (Wilcoxon)

Subjects	Condition 1 (without music)	Condition 2 (music)	d	Ranks of d	Signed ranks (plus)	Signed ranks (minus)
1	3	5	−2	−5		(−)5
2	4	5	−1	−2		(−)2
3	3	2	+1	+2	(+)2	
4	1	5	−4	−8.5		(−)8.5
5	5	4	+1	+2	(+)2	
6	2	5	−3	−7		(−)7
7	3	5	−2	−5		(−)5
8	4	4	0	(tie)		
9	1	5	−4	−8.5		(−)8.5
10	3	5	−2	−5		(−)5
Means	2.9	4.5		Rank totals	(+)4	(−)41

Rationale

The experimental design is *related* because the same subjects performed under both conditions. This means that it is possible to compare the pairs of scores produced by each subject and to calculate the differences in the scores for each subject between the two conditions. The aim of the Wilcoxon test is to compare the performance of subjects to find out whether there are significant differences between their scores in the two conditions.

In Table 6.1 the scores for condition 2 are subtracted from these for condition 1. These differences *d* are given a plus or, if negative, a minus sign. The differences are then ranked (disregarding plus or minus signs). Once all the differences have been ranked, the original signs are assigned to the ranks (signed ranks) as shown in the columns labelled 'Signed ranks (plus)' and 'Signed ranks (minus)'. The next step is to add up the totals of the signed ranks. In this case the two plus signs add up to 4 and the seven minus signs add up to 41. The statistic *W* is calculated as the smaller rank total, in this case the total of the plus signed ranks.

If you look back to the experimental hypothesis, you will see that the prediction was that subjects would recall more words in condition 2 (with music) than in condition 1 (without music). It is not surprising that if one subtracts the better scores in condition 2 from the less good scores in condition 1 one is bound to end up with a lot of minuses. So the fact that there are a lot of minuses supports the hypothesis. It is just a statistical convention that the *smaller* total of signed ranks is used to calculate the statistic *W*.

Box A

Step-by-step instructions for calculating the value of W

1	Calculate the difference (d) between each pair of scores, assigning plus or minus signs.	Subtract condition 2 from condition 1: see the d column in Table 6.1.
2	Rank the differences (d) from the smallest (rank 1) to the largest. When ranking *omit* tied scores and *ignore* the plus and minus signs.	See the 'Ranks of d' column in Table 6.1.
3	Assign plus and minus signs to the ranks in the 'Signed ranks' columns.	See plus and minus signs in 'Signed ranks (plus)' and 'Signed ranks (minus)' columns in Table 6.1.
4	Add the rank totals for signed ranks (plus) and signed ranks (minus) separately.	Rank total (plus) = (+)4 Rank total (minus) = (−)41
5	Take the smaller rank total as W.	$W = 4$
6	Note the number of subjects N (not counting ties).	$N = 10 - 1\,\text{tie} = 9$

All the ranks have to be plus or minus. So, if the plus signs are small enough to be significant, the minus signs must also be significantly large.

Step-by-step instructions for calculating the value of W

These are given in Box A.

Looking up the significance of W in Table A

Table A in Appendix 2 gives the levels of significance for testing one-tailed and two-tailed hypotheses. The experimental hypothesis was a one-tailed prediction that listening to music would improve recall of words. The next step is to look up the appropriate N, which refers to the number of subjects. There were ten subjects but only nine showed a difference between the conditions. Subject 8 was a tie and so is omitted from the analysis because it cannot be ranked as a plus or a minus. So $N = 9$.

Since the convention is to take the *smaller* total of signed ranks, the calculated value of W has to be *equal to* or *less than* the values of W in

Table A. For $N = 9$ the calculated W of 4 is smaller than the value of 6 in the second column. If you look at the top of the table the level of significance for a one-tailed test is $p < 0.025$. Since this is an acceptable level of significance, the null hypothesis can be rejected.

? Question 14 Is the significance level of $p < 0.025$ more significant than

(a) $p < 0.05$

(b) $p < 0.001$

Conclusions

Looking back at the means in Table 6.1, the results show that subjects recall more words when music is playing than without music ($p < 0.025$).

? Question 15 To test the effects of sentence length on comprehension, eight subjects were each asked to read two texts matched for content difficulty. In one of the texts ideas were expressed in short, precise sentences; in the other, ideas were expressed in long, complex sentences. The experimental hypothesis predicted that comprehension scores would be higher for short-sentence texts. The results are shown in Table 6.2.

Table 6.2 Comprehension scores

Subjects	Condition 1 (short sentences)	Condition 2 (long sentences)	d	Ranks of d	Signed ranks (plus)	Signed ranks (minus)
1	7	8				
2	10	6				
3	13	4				
4	8	4				
5	7	7				
6	8	10				
7	6	3				
8	10	3				
Means				Rank totals		

(a) Calculate the mean scores for the two conditions to two decimal places.

(b) Following the step-by-step instructions in Box A, complete the blank columns in Table 6.2. Is W significant and, if so, at what level of significance?

(c) What precautions would the experimenter have to take when designing this experiment as a related design using same subjects?

| 6.2 | Mann–Whitney test (unrelated) |

When to use

The Mann–Whitney test should be used for an *unrelated design* when different subjects are used in *two conditions*.

Sample data

A researcher was interested in whether people would find it easier to remember a passage of text if they are given a relevant title. One group of subjects was given a relevant title before reading a text. A second group of subjects was given no title before reading the text. All subjects were tested for their memory of the text. The results are shown in Table 6.3.

Table 6.3 Recall scores for texts with and without a title (Mann–Whitney)

	Condition 1 (no title)	Overall ranks (ranks 1)	Condition 2 (title)	Overall ranks (ranks 2)
	3	3	9	13
	4	4	7	10.5
	2	1.5	5	6
	6	8.5	10	14
	2	1.5	6	8.5
	5	6	8	12
			5	6
			7	10.5
Rank totals		$T_1 = 24.5$		$T_2 = 80.5$
Means	3.67		7.13	

Hypothesis

The prediction was that the group of subjects who were given a relevant title before learning the text (condition 2) would remember the text better than the group of subjects given no title (condition 1).

? **Question 16** Why is it better to use different subjects in each condition to test this hypothesis?

? **Question 17** Is it possible to have different numbers of subjects in a related design?

Rationale

The rationale behind the Mann–Whitney test is very similar to that of the Wilcoxon test. The basic difference between the two tests is between a related design using the same subjects and an unrelated design using different subjects. The Wilcoxon test analyses the differences between the performance of the *same* subjects under two experimental conditions. The Mann–Whitney test analyses differences between conditions for *different* groups of subjects. In this case, each subject produces a score in only one condition. So it is *not* possible to compare pairs of scores for each subject. Instead all the scores have to be ranked across both conditions as an *overall* set of ranks (see Chapter 5, Section 5.4). It is only after all the ranks have been ranked together that the totals of ranks are added up separately for condition 1 and condition 2, as shown in the Ranks (1) and Ranks (2) columns in Table 6.3.

If the differences between conditions are random differences, as stated by the null hypothesis, there should be roughly equal ranks in the two conditions. If there is a large preponderance of low or high ranks in one condition or the other, the differences between conditions are likely to be due to the predicted effects of the independent variable. If the sum of ranks for one of the conditions is very small then there must be a preponderance of high ranks in the other condition. A statistic called U reflects the smaller sum of ranks. As with the Wilcoxon, it is a convention that the smaller value of U represents a higher probability of a significant difference between the two conditions.

Step-by-step instructions for calculating the value of U

These are given in Box B.

 Box B

Step-by-step instructions for calculating the value of U

1   Rank *all* the scores (taking both groups together as an *overall* set of ranks), giving rank 1 to the lowest score in the usual way.

     See overall ranks for both conditions taken together in Table 6.3.

2   After ranking all the scores, add the rank totals for each condition.

     $T_1 = 24.5$
     $T_2 = 80.5$

3   Calculate U using the formula:

$$U = n_1 n_2 + \frac{n_1(n_1 + 1)}{2} - T_1$$

     $$U = 6 \times 8 + \frac{6(6 + 1)}{2} - 24.5$$

$$= 48 + \frac{42}{2} - 24.5$$

$$= 48 + 21 - 24.5$$

$$= 44.5$$

   n_1 = number of subjects in condition 1
   n_2 = number of subjects in condition 2
   T_1 = rank total for condition 1

     $n_1 = 6$
     $n_2 = 8$
     $T_1 = 24.5$

4   Next substitute the values of U, n_1 and n_2 in the following formula and calculate U^1

   $U^1 = n_1 n_2 - U$

     $U^1 = 6 \times 8 - 44.5$
     $= 3.5$

5   Take the smaller value of U or U^1 as U

     $U = 3.5$

Looking up the significance of U in Table B

It may seem very daunting to have to look up U in four separate tables. The reason is that you have to look up the numbers of subjects in both conditions (in case these are different). In Table B(1) the number of subjects in the first condition (n_1) is listed along the top and the number of subjects in the second condition (n_2) is listed in the first column. In the sample experiment there are six subjects in condition 1 and eight subjects in condition 2, so $n_1 = 6$ and $n_2 = 8$.

But how do we know which of Tables B(1)–B(4) we should consult to test the significance levels of the calculated U? These tables give you the critical values of U at different levels of significance for one-tailed and two-tailed tests for different combinations of n_1 and n_2 for the two groups. You have to locate the appropriate table.

The usual procedure is to start with Table B(4), which gives the values of U for $p < 0.05$ for a one-tailed test. In Table B(4) locate $n_1 = 6$ along the top and $n_2 = 8$ down the side and at the intersection you will find a value of U which is 10. Since it is a convention to use the smaller value of U, the calculated value of $U = 3.5$ must be *equal to* or *less than* the critical value of 10, which it is. The next step is to move to Table B(3) to see whether the calculated value of U is significant at a more stringent level of significance. In Table B(3) the calculated value of 3.5 is smaller than the value of 8 for $n_1 = 6$ and $n_2 = 8$. Moving on to Table B(2), the calculated value of $U = 3.5$ is smaller than 6 for $n_1 = 6$ and $n_2 = 8$. Finally, in Table B(1), the calculated value of $U = 3.5$ is smaller than the value of 4 for $n_1 = 6$, $n_2 = 8$.

As the experimental hypothesis was one-tailed, the null hypothesis can be rejected ($p < 0.005$). This represents a very low probability of a random result of 5 in 1000. If the hypothesis had been two-tailed, the random probability in Table B(1) would have been $p < 0.01$, a less extreme probability of 1 in 100.

Conclusions

It is essential to refer back to the means in Table 6.3 to check whether the results are significant in the predicted direction. Since the means show a difference in favour of condition 2 it can be concluded that the prediction that subjects remember more of a text when given an appropriate title was supported ($p < 0.005$).

? Question 18 Twenty six-letter words were presented at a very fast level of exposure on a screen to two groups of different subjects. For one group the words were all presented on the left-hand side of the screen. For the other group the words were all presented on the right-hand side of the screen. The experimenter was interested in testing the effects of the direction of reading (left to right in our culture) on subjects' ability to recognize words which are flashed up only for a brief moment. The results are shown in Table 6.4. The experimental hypothesis stated that subjects given the words on the left-hand side of the screen would recognize more words.

(a) Is this experimental design a related design or an unrelated design?

(b) Calculate the mean scores for each group.

(c) Is the experimental hypothesis one-tailed or two-tailed?

(d) Complete the overall ranks and the rank totals in Table 6.4 and use the Mann–Whitney test to analyse the significance of the results.

(e) Is the experimental hypothesis supported by these results?

Table 6.4 Number of words recognized for left-hand and right-hand presentation

Condition 1 Right-hand presentation	Overall ranks (ranks 1)	Condition 2 Left-hand presentation	Overall ranks (ranks 2)
17		18	
13		15	
12		17	
16		13	
10		11	
15		16	
11		10	
13		17	
12			
Rank totals	$T_1 =$		$T_2 =$
Means			

7 Non-parametric tests (three or more conditions)

7.1 Friedman test (related)

When to use

The Friedman test should be used for a *related design* when the same subjects are used for *three or more conditions*.

Sample data

Suppose a publisher producing a series of children's books wants to choose from three types of illustrations the one which is most appealing to children. Eight children are asked to rate all three illustrations on a five-point scale. The children were presented with the three illustrations in different orders. The rating scores for the three illustrations are shown in Table 7.1.

Question 19 Why were the illustrations presented in different orders?

Hypothesis

The experimenter predicted that children would rate some illustrations as being more appealing than others.

Table 7.1   Rating scores for three illustrations (Friedman)

Subjects	Condition 1 (illustration A)		Condition 2 (illustration B)		Condition 3 (illustration C)	
	Rating scores	Ranks	Rating scores	Ranks	Rating scores	Ranks
1	2	1	5	3	4	2
2	1	1	5	3	3	2
3	3	1	5	2.5	5	2.5
4	3	2	5	3	2	1
5	2	1	3	2	5	3
6	1	1	4	2.5	4	2.5
7	5	3	3	2	2	1
8	1	1	4	3	3	2
Rank totals		11		21		16
Means	2.25		4.25		3.50	

Rationale

Since this is a related design in which each subject produces rating scores for all conditions, it is possible to compare scores for each subject *across* conditions to see under which conditions they produce small or large rating scores. Because there are more than two conditions, it is not possible to calculate differences between the scores for two conditions as was the case with the Wilcoxon test. Instead we rank-order the scores for each subject *horizontally* across the rows for the three conditions. For example, in Table 7.1, subject 1's rating scores of 2 for condition 1, 5 for condition 2 and 4 for condition 3 are assigned three ranks from smallest to largest: rank 1 for condition 1, rank 2 for condition 3 and rank 3 for condition 2; and similarly for the other subjects. Of course, if there were *four* experimental conditions the scores would be ranked for each subject from 1 to 4. This *horizontal ranking* is the most difficult concept for the Friedman test. Remember the aim is to compare the three scores produced by each subject doing all three conditions.

The next step is to add up the totals of ranks for each condition. If there are only random differences between the rating scores for all three conditions, as stated by the null hypothesis, we would expect the rank totals to be approximately equal, since there would be some low ranks (low scores) and some high ranks (high scores) in each of the conditions. However, if the conditions are significantly different, we would expect to get quite different rank totals, with some conditions having a preponderance of low ranks and some a preponderance of high ranks. The size of the difference between rank totals is given by a statistic called χ^2_r (pronounced 'ky-R-square').

Step-by-step instructions for calculating the value of χ^2_r

Before starting on the step-by-step instructions in Box C (overleaf), we need to introduce some new terms.

The symbol Σ (pronounced *sigma*) means to add up all the numbers which come after the symbol. Σ is the Greek letter S, which stands for 'sum'. Instead of saying 'add up a total' it is more usual to say 'sum numbers' to produce a *sum* (another word for total).

The other requirement is to square numbers, which just means multiply a number by itself, for example 2^2 is $2 \times 2 = 4$. For the calculation of χ^2_r you will have to square the rank totals and sum them (ΣT^2). None of this is as difficult as it seems.

Looking up the significance of χ^2_r in Table C

There are two tables to look up the critical values of χ^2_r. Table C(1) gives χ^2_r values for three conditions when N (number of subjects) is between 2 and 9. Table C(2) gives χ^2_r values for four conditions when N equals 2, 3 or 4. If the calculated χ^2_r is *equal to* or *larger than* the values in Tables C(1) or C(2), this indicates that the differences in total ranks between the conditions are large enough to be significant.

The table you should consult to look up the calculated value of χ^2_r for the sample experiment is Table C(1) because *eight* subjects are performing under *three* conditions. Locate the appropriate column for N and find in the p column the nearest probability which is less than one of the conventional levels of significance. The calculated value of $\chi^2_r = 6.25$ for eight subjects is equivalent to a probability of $p < 0.047$. We hope you can see that this probability is less than $p < 0.05$, one of the conventional levels of significance.

Conclusions

The children gave significantly different ratings to the illustrations ($p < 0.05$). It appears from the means in Table 7.1 that they preferred illustration B, since this received the highest ratings, with illustration C next and illustration A last. However, the Friedman test can only test for overall differences between conditions (the equivalent of a two-tailed hypothesis). To see if there is a *trend* in favour of the illustrations in a particular order you would need to use Page's L trend test.

Box C

Step-by-step instructions for calculating the value of χ_r^2

1   Rank the scores for each *separate* subject *horizontally across* each row, giving 1 to the smallest score, 2 to the next score and 3 to the highest score.

     See 'Ranks' columns in Table 7.1 allocating ranks 1, 2, 3 for each subject (sometimes tied, e.g. 2.5 for subjects 3 and 6).

2   Calculate the rank totals for each condition.

     $T_1 = 11$, $T_2 = 21$, $T_3 = 16$

3   Note the following symbols:

     number of conditions (C) $C = 3$

     number of subjects (N) $N = 8$

     T^2 = squares of rank totals

$$T_1^2 = 11 \times 11 = 121$$
$$T_2^2 = 21 \times 21 = 441$$
$$T_3^2 = 16 \times 16 = 256$$
$$\Sigma T^2 = 11^2 + 21^2 + 16^2 = 818$$

4   Calculate the value of χ_r^2 using the formula

$$\chi_r^2 = \left[\frac{12}{NC(C+1)} \Sigma T^2 \right] - 3N(C+1)$$

$$\chi_r^2 = \left[\left(\frac{12}{(8 \times 3)(3 + 1)} \right) (11^2 + 21^2 + 16^2) \right] - 3 \times 8(3 + 1)$$

$$= \left[\left(\frac{12}{24 \times 4} \right) (121 + 441 + 256) \right] - (24 \times 4)$$

$$= \left[\frac{12}{96} \times 818 \right] - 96$$

$$= 102.25 - 96$$

$$= 6.25$$

?   **Question 20**   Five subjects were given three passages of prose to read, one typed in black print, one in red print and one in green print. Scores were the number of ideas recalled, as shown in Table 7.2.

Table 7.2 Number of ideas recalled

Subjects	Condition 1 (black print)	Condition 2 (red print)	Condition 3 (green print)
1	4	5	6
2	2	7	7
3	6	6	8
4	3	7	5
5	3	8	9

(a) What are the mean scores for the three conditions?

(b) What is the independent variable and what is the dependent variable?

(c) What is the appropriate statistical test and why?

(d) Following the step-by-step instructions in Box C, work out the ranks and rank totals and calculate χ_r^2.

(e) What conclusions can be drawn from this experiment?

7.2 Page's *L* trend test (related)

When to use

This test can be thought of as an extension of the Friedman test, when you need to look at whether there is a *trend* between *three or more conditions*. It should be used for a *related design* when the same subjects are doing all conditions.

Sample data

We shall use the same example as that for the Friedman test. From the results of such an experiment we might wish to predict that there is a significant *trend* in the children's ratings for each illustration in the order of greatest preference for illustration B, followed by illustrations C and A. In order to test this we *rearrange* the order of conditions from the lowest to the highest predicted ratings. This means that the original order of conditions 1, 2, 3 in Table 7.1 becomes 1, 3, 2, indicating a predicted order from lowest to highest rating scores. Table 7.3 shows the rating scores in the new order from lowest to highest.

Table 7.3   Rating scores for three illustrations in predicted order (Page's L)

Subjects	Condition 1 (same) (illustration A) Rating scores	Ranks	Condition 2 (old 3) (illustration C) Rating scores	Ranks	Condition 3 (old 2) (illustration B) Rating scores	Ranks
1	2	1	4	2	5	3
2	1	1	3	2	5	3
3	3	1	5	2.5	5	2.5
4	3	2	2	1	5	3
5	2	1	5	3	3	2
6	1	1	4	2.5	4	2.5
7	5	3	2	1	3	2
8	1	1	3	2	4	3
Rank totals		11		16		21
Means	2.25		3.50		4.25	

Hypothesis

On the basis of previous research, the experimenter predicted that illustration A would have the lowest ratings, illustration C the next lowest ratings and illustration B the highest ratings.

Rationale

The rationale behind the test is exactly the same as that for the Friedman test, except that this time we are predicting that the rank totals will fall in a certain *order*, from the *smallest* on the left to the *largest* on the right-hand side of the table. It is important to remember that the conditions should appear in the predicted order from the group whose scores are predicted to be the lowest on the left to the group whose scores are predicted to be the largest on the right.

As with the Friedman test, you should start by ranking the three conditions for each subject *horizontally* across conditions. The next step is to add up the rank totals for each condition. If there are random differences between the conditions, as stated by the null hypothesis, we would expect the rank totals to be approximately equal, since there would be some high ranks and some low ranks in each of the conditions. However, if there is

Box D

Step-by-step instructions for calculating the value of L

1	Rank the scores for each *separate* subject *horizontally across* each row (as with the Friedman test).	See 'Ranks' columns in Table 7.3, allocating ranks 1, 2, 3 across the three conditions for each subject, allowing for ties.
2	Calculate the rank totals for each condition.	$T_1 = 11$, $T_2 = 16$, $T_3 = 21$
3	Note the following symbols:	
	c = numbers allotted to the conditions 1, 2, 3 from left to right	
	$(T \times c)$ = the rank total for each condition multiplied by its respective condition number	$T_1 \times 1 = 11 \times 1$ $T_2 \times 2 = 16 \times 2$ $T_3 \times 3 = 21 \times 3$
	Number of conditions (C)	$C = 3$
	Number of subjects (N)	$N = 8$
4	Calculate L using the formula	
	$L = \sum(T \times c)$	$L = (11 \times 1) + (16 \times 2) + (21 \times 3)$ $= 11 + 32 + 63$ $= 106$

a significant trend in scores, we would expect the rank totals to occur in the predicted order from the smallest rank total on the left to the highest on the right.

Step-by-step instructions for calculating the value of L

These are given in Box D.

Looking up the significance of L in Table D

The trend in rank totals is given by a statistic called L. Since L reflects the size of the differences between rank totals in the predicted direction the value of L should be *equal to* or *larger than* the values in Table D.

The value of L is dependent upon the number of subjects and the number of conditions (3 to 6). When you refer to Table D locate the number of conditions (*C*) used in your experiment (in our example 3) along the top row of the table and the number of subjects (*N*) (in our example 8) down the left-hand column. At the intersection of the *N* row and the *C* column you will find the critical value of *L* for three levels of significance in the final column of Table D. The upper figure in each group gives the value of *L* for $p < 0.001$, the middle figure gives *L* for $p < 0.01$ and the lower figure gives *L* for $p < 0.05$. In our example, the calculated value of $L = 106$ is equal to the value for 8 subjects at the $p < 0.01$ level of significance. Note that Page's *L* trend test is equivalent to a one-tailed test because it tests a trend in one direction, predicting a specific order of conditions.

Conclusions

The children rated the illustrations in the predicted order, illustration A had the lowest ratings, illustration C next lowest and illustration A the highest ($p < 0.01$).

Question 21 Five subjects were given three texts to read and were told that they would be asked for verbatim recall. In condition 1 the sentences were short; in condition 2 the sentences were of medium length; and in condition 3 the sentences were long. The experimenter predicted that the number of correct sentences recalled would decrease across the three conditions, from most sentences recalled in condition 1, to significantly fewer in condition 2 and fewest in condition 3. Results are shown in Table 7.4.

Table 7.4 Number of sentences recalled

Subjects	Condition 1 (short sentences)	Condition 2 (medium length sentences)	Condition 3 (long sentences)
1	8	7	3
2	10	5	3
3	9	2	4
4	7	4	1
5	11	5	6
Means	9	4.6	3.4

(a) How should the conditions be ordered in order to use Page's trend test to test the predicted trend?

(b) Calculate *L* to test whether the results support the predicted trend.

7.3	**Kruskal–Wallis test (unrelated)**

When to use

The Kruskal–Wallis test should be used for an *unrelated design* when different subjects are used for *three or more* conditions.

Sample data

Suppose a researcher is interested in finding out whether there are significant differences in the learning of three types of texts: highly illustrated, with some illustrations or no illustrations. Different subjects are assigned to each of the three experimental conditions and the dependent variable is the number of ideas recalled from each text, as shown in Table 7.5.

Hypothesis

The prediction was that the number of illustrations would affect subjects' recall of ideas from the text.

Rationale

The aim of the test is to determine whether scores for three or more groups of subjects are significantly different. Because the scores come from *different* subjects the only way to look at differences between conditions

Table 7.5 Number of ideas recalled for illustrated texts (Kruskal–Wallis)

	Condition 1 (highly illustrated text)		Condition 2 (text with some illustrations)		Condition 3 (text with no illustrations)	
	Scores	*Ranks*	*Scores*	*Ranks*	*Scores*	*Ranks*
	19	10	14	6	12	3.5
	21	11	15	7	12	3.5
	17	9	9	1	13	5
	16	8			10	2
Rank totals		38		14		14
Means	18.25		12.67		11.75	

is to rank all the scores together as an *overall* set of ranks, as with the Mann–Whitney test. The overall ranks are added up for each condition separately to produce a rank total for each condition. If there are only random differences between the conditions, as stated by the null hypothesis, we would expect high and low ranks to be spread roughly equally among the conditions. But, if there is a preponderance of high or low ranks in one or other of the different conditions, it is more likely that these reflect significant differences due to the independent variable.

Step-by-step instructions for calculating the value of *H*

In order to calculate *H* you will have to square the rank totals, divide them by the number of subjects and sum these. If you are unsure about any of the symbols used in Box E, refer back to the instructions for calculating the Friedman statistic in Section 7.1.

Looking up the significance of *H* in Tables E and F

The differences between rank totals is calculated as a statistic called *H*. Since the experimental hypothesis predicts that there will be large differences between conditions, the observed value of *H* should be *equal to* or *larger than* the values in Tables E and F in order to be significant.

Table E covers experiments for *three* groups of subjects with *up to five* subjects in each group. In the left-hand column of Table E you will see the numbers of subjects for each group when no more than three groups are being tested. Locate the relevant combination (in Table 7.3 the number of subjects in condition 1 is 4, in condition 2 there are 3, and in condition 3 there are 4 subjects). Remember that it is possible to have unequal numbers of subjects in each condition when different groups of subjects are doing each condition. Note also that the *order* of the numbers of subjects for each group does not matter. In the sample experiment the group sizes were $n_1 = 4$, $n_2 = 3$ and $n_3 = 4$. But the appropriate combination in Table E is 4, 4, 3. Against this combination of group sizes you will find critical values of *H* for various probabilities. In our example, the calculated value of $H = 7.2$ for group sizes 4, 4, 3 is larger than the critical value of 7.1439 for $p < 0.01$, so we can accept the experimental hypothesis at this level of significance.

If you have *more than three* conditions and/or *more than five* subjects per condition, you will have to look up the probabilities of *H* in another table, Table F, known as 'chi-square' (pronounced 'ky-square'). This table is designed for the chi-square test which you will come across in Chapter 9.

Box E

Step-by-step instructions for calculating the value of *H*

1   Rank *all* the scores *across* conditions as an *overall* set of ranks, giving 1 to the smallest score and so on.

See the 'Ranks' columns in Table 7.5 which contain the overall ranks of all scores taken together

2   Calculate rank totals for each condition.

$T_1 = 38$, $T_2 = 14$, $T_3 = 14$

3   Note the following symbols:

     N = total number of subjects

     $N = 11$

     n = number of subjects in each group

     $n_1 = 4$, $n_2 = 3$, $n_3 = 4$

     T^2 = squares of the rank totals for each condition

     $T_1^2 = 38^2$, $T_2^2 = 14^2$, $T_3^2 = 14^2$

     $\dfrac{\sum T^2}{n}$ = sum of the squared rank totals for each condition divided by the number of subjects in that condition

$$H = \left[\frac{12}{N(N+1)} \sum \frac{T^2}{n} \right] - 3(N+1)$$

$$H = \left[\frac{12}{11 \times 12} \left(\frac{38^2}{4} + \frac{14^2}{3} + \frac{14^2}{4} \right) \right]$$
$$- 3 \times 12$$

$$= \left[\frac{12}{132} \left(\frac{1444}{4} + \frac{196}{3} + \frac{196}{4} \right) \right] - 36$$
$$= 0.091(361 + 65.33 + 49) - 36$$
$$= 43.2 - 36$$
$$= 7.2$$

4   Calculate the degrees of freedom: the number of conditions (*C*) minus one.

$df = C - 1$
$= 3 - 1$
$= 2$

As an example, we will look up the calculated $H = 7.2$ in Table F. In order to look up probabilities in Table F you have to calculate what you will later learn about as 'degrees of freedom'. For now simply take it on trust that *df* in the first column of Table F is calculated as $C - 1$, the number of conditions minus 1. In this case, with three conditions, $C - 1 = 2$.

Now turn to Table F. The significance levels are given at the top of the table. Looking across the row for $df = 2$, the calculated $H = 7.2$ is larger than the value of 5.99 for $p < 0.05$.

Conclusions

On the basis of the probabilities in Table E, subjects were influenced by the number of illustrations in the texts ($p < 0.01$). It appears from the means in Table 7.5 that subjects recalled more ideas from the highly illustrated text, fewer ideas from the text with some illustrations and the fewest ideas from the text with no illustrations. The Kruskal–Wallis can only test whether there are overall differences between conditions (the equivalent of a two-tailed hypothesis). To see whether there is a *trend* you will need to use the Jonckheere trend test.

? Question 22 An experimenter wanted to investigate the effect that different types of instructions have on solving problems. One group of subjects was given written instructions. A second group of subjects was shown how the puzzle was solved but had no written instructions. The third group of subjects was given written instructions and also shown how to solve the puzzle. The three groups were then asked to solve the puzzle. Scores were obtained by counting the number of wrong moves, i.e. errors made, as shown in Table 7.6.

(a) What are the mean error scores for each group?

(b) Fill in the ranks and calculate H. Is the calculated value of H significant?

(c) What conclusions can be drawn about the relative difficulty of the three conditions?

Table 7.6 Number of errors made in solving a puzzle

Condition 1 (instructions only)	Condition 2 (shown solution, no instructions)	Condition 3 (instructions and shown solution)
20	25	19
27	33	20
19	35	25
23	36	22

(d) Would there have been any problems in carrying out this experiment using a related design with the same subjects doing all conditions?

(e) Suppose there were eight subjects in each of four conditions and that the calculated value of H was 12.50. Using Table F, what would be the appropriate significance level? Remember the degrees of freedom (df) is the number of conditions minus 1.

7.4 Jonckheere trend test (unrelated)

When to use

The Jonckheere trend test can be thought of as an extension of the Kruskal–Wallis test for looking at *trends* between *three or more* conditions. It should be used for an *unrelated* design when *different* subjects are doing each of the conditions.

Sample data

We shall use the example worked out for the Kruskal–Wallis test when we tested the learning of three different types of illustrated texts, allocating different subjects to each text. Suppose that this time we predict that subjects' scores will show a *trend* so that they recall a significantly greater number of ideas from the highly illustrated texts, fewer ideas from the text with some illustrations and fewest ideas from the non-illustrated text.

Because we are predicting a trend in that direction, we have to rearrange the experimental conditions from left to right to give the order of no illustrations (which is predicted to produce the lowest scores), some illustrations next and finally highly illustrated (which should produce the highest scores). Notice that this is opposite to the way we had the conditions in Table 7.5. It is a general convention with trend tests to order the conditions in the predicted order from lowest scores on the left to highest on the right. As is often the case, it is advisable to have equal numbers of subjects under each condition, and for the Jonckheere test it is essential. We have therefore assumed that four subjects were tested in each of the three conditions, so that condition 2 has an extra subject in Table 7.7 as compared with Table 7.5.

Table 7.7 Number of ideas recalled for illustrated texts (Jonckheere)

	Condition 1 (old 3) (text with no illustrations)	Condition 2 (old 2) (text with some illustrations)	Condition 3 (old 1) (highly illustrated text)
	12 (7)	14 (4)	19
	12 (7)	15 (4)	21
	13 (6)	9 (4)	17
	10 (7)	13 (4)	16
Means	11.75	12.75	18.25

Hypothesis

On the basis of previous research the experimenter predicted that the more illustrations there are in a text the easier it is to recall ideas from the text.

Rationale

The rationale behind the Jonckheere trend test is completely different from those so far described. Scores are *not ranked*. Instead what the test does is to count the number of scores which are higher in each condition than scores in previous conditions. If there are only random differences, as stated by the null hypothesis, the scores in each condition should be roughly equal and there should be no reason for the scores in any of the conditions to be higher than in the others. But, if there is a preponderance of scores that are higher in the right-hand columns, this means that there is a trend from lowest scores on the left to highest scores on the right, as predicted by the experimental hypothesis. Any preponderance of higher scores in the right-hand conditions is given by a statistic called S. Once you have got the hang of the Jonckheere test it is one of the easiest tests to calculate.

Step-by-step instructions for calculating the value of S

These are given in Box F.

Looking up the significance of S in Table G

Table G gives you critical values of S depending on the number of subjects in each condition (n up to 10) and number of conditions (C 3 to 6) for two levels of significance ($p < 0.05$ and $p < 0.01$). If the calculated value of S

Box F

Step-by-step instructions for calculating the value of *S*

1   Starting with the left-hand condition, for *each separate score* count up the number of scores in all the conditions to the *right* of condition 1 which are higher than that score. Do *not* include ties across conditions when calculating the numbers of higher scores. Do the same for the scores in condition 2.

The numbers in brackets in Table 7.7 represent the numbers of right-hand higher scores for each score in condition 1 and condition 2. Condition 3 has no scores to the right of it.

2   Add up the sum of the figures in brackets. Call this sum *A*.

$$A = 7 + 7 + 6 + 7 + 4 + 4 + 4 + 4$$
$$= 43$$

C = number of conditions

$$C = 3$$

n = number of subjects in each condition

$$n = 4$$

3   Calculate *B* using the formula:

$$B = \frac{C(C-1)}{2} \times n^2$$

$$B = \frac{3(3-1)}{2} \times 4^2$$

$$= \frac{3 \times 2}{2} \times 16$$

$$= 3 \times 16$$

$$= 48$$

4   Calculate the value of *S* by substituting *A* and *B* in the formula:

$$S = 2A - B$$

$$S = (2 \times 43) - 48$$

$$= 86 - 48$$

$$= 38$$

is *equal to* or *larger than* the value for a particular level of significance, you can reject the null hypothesis. For $n = 4$ and $C = 3$ our calculated value of $S = 38$ is *larger* than the value of 24 for $p < 0.05$. We now look at the critical value for $p < 0.01$ and find that the calculated S of 38 is greater than the critical value of 32 for this level of significance. So we can reject the null hypothesis at the $p < 0.01$ level of significance. Note that the Jonckheere trend test is equivalent to a *one-tailed test* because it tests a trend in one particular direction, not in both directions.

Conclusions

The results supported the prediction that the recall of ideas for the text with no illustrations would be lowest, with some illustrations recall would be improved and that most ideas would be recalled from highly illustrated texts ($p < 0.01$).

? Question 23 A researcher predicted that most words would be recalled from lists of very common words, fewer from fairly common words and fewest from a list of uncommon words. The recall scores are shown in Table 7.8.

Table 7.8 Recall of lists of words

Condition 1 (very common words)	Condition 2 (fairly common words)	Condition 3 (uncommon words)
14	7	2
15	8	4
10	3	4
13	2	2

(a) Work out the means for each condition.

(b) Put the conditions in order from smallest to largest scores.

(c) Carry out the step-by-step instructions for the Jonckheere test.

(d) Does the calculated S show a significant trend?

8 Correlations

8.1 Interpreting correlations

The non-parametric tests discussed so far have predicted *differences* between experimental conditions. Whether the same or different subjects have been used, the researcher has manipulated an independent variable to test its effect on subjects' performances.

There are times, however, when experimenters are less interested in predicting differences in behaviour as a result of an independent variable. Instead they want to investigate whether variables are *associated* together. Consider again the relationship between the variables of spelling ability and reading scores. A researcher might predict that over the whole range of spelling ability and reading ability children who are good spellers will also tend to score highly on a reading test, while children at the bottom end of the spelling scale will not do so well at reading.

All the children would be given a spelling test and a reading test. But this time *neither of the variables will be the independent or the dependent variable*. The researcher will take measures of both variables in order to see whether those children who score highly on spelling also score highly on a reading test, while children who score less well on spelling also score less well on the reading test. This is known as a **correlational design**. The aim is to test the hypothesis that children's performance on one variable (spelling) *correlates* with their performance on another variable (reading).

There is one point you should notice about a correlational design. Because neither of the variables is being manipulated by the experimenter, it is not possible to predict which variable is having an effect on the other variable. All one can say is that there is a relationship between the two variables. For instance, it would be possible to give plausible arguments in favour of quite different relationships between spelling ability and the likelihood of benefiting from a reading scheme.

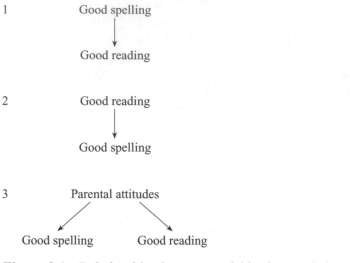

Figure 8.1   Relationships between variables in correlations

1 Spelling ability aids reading.
2 Being a good reader improves spelling.
3 Both good spelling and good reading are the result of some other variable altogether, e.g. a positive attitude by parents towards school lessons.

The point of the examples in Figure 8.1 is that it demonstrates that it is not possible to identify the *cause* of a correlation. It may be extremely likely that a correlation represents a causal explanation. The strong and consistent correlations between smoking and lung cancer have led to acceptance of a causal connection. But in principle it is possible that there is some common factor affecting the use of cigarettes and a predisposition to lung cancer. That is why medical research has been undertaken to discover mechanisms which would indicate a direct causal link.

Correlational designs are often used in educational research where it is often impossible to vary conditions for ethical reasons. Depriving children of good teachers is not an acceptable option. One example might be a researcher studying the arithmetic abilities and the reading abilities of children by giving them arithmetic and reading tests. The aim is to discover whether children who obtain high arithmetic scores also obtain high reading scores. The question at issue is whether reading ability and being good at arithmetic 'go together' or whether there is no connection between the two kinds of ability.

Children's scores on an arithmetic test and a reading test are shown in Table 8.1. It would be possible to test whether there are differences in arithmetic and reading performance by comparing the means for the two conditions. But this would be an unlikely hypothesis. What would be the

Table 8.1 Arithmetic scores (out of 20) and reading scores (out of 10)

Child	Arithmetic scores	Reading scores
1	20	10
2	18	9
3	16	8
4	14	7
5	12	6
6	10	5
7	8	4
8	6	3
9	4	2
10	2	1

basis for predicting that children are better at arithmetic than reading? It is more reasonable to investigate whether children who are good at reading are also good at other subjects like arithmetic; in other words, to test whether there is a correlation between arithmetic and reading scores.

Question 24 (a) What would be three possible explanations if a significant correlation was found between arithmetic and reading? Look at the example for spelling and reading in Figure 8.1.

(b) What would be a likely explanation for a correlation between a cock crowing and an alarm clock going off?

8.2 Positive correlations

The next question that needs to be asked is whether the two sets of scores are likely to be correlated. Look carefully at the scores in Table 8.1. Child 1 is top at both spelling and reading and child 2 is next best at both. Check each child's score for spelling and reading, right down to the unfortunate child 10 who gets the lowest scores on both tests. In a case like this, it can be claimed that spelling and reading scores are highly correlated. Because the variables move in the *same direction*, this is known as a **positive correlation**. High scores on spelling 'go together' with high scores on reading, medium scores go with medium scores and low scores go with low scores.

Question 25 Which of the following are most likely to result in a high positive correlation? Which are not likely to be correlated at all?

(a) Height and shoe size.

(b) Number of cinema tickets sold and the number of customers in the audience.

(c) Amount of spinach eaten and size of wins on football pools.

It is obvious from the examples in Question 25 that in some cases positive correlations between pairs of scores are likely to be high while relationships between other pairs of scores are likely to produce a much lower amount of correlation, or no correlation at all, as in the case of completely unrelated variables like eating spinach and winning the pools. Another way of putting this is that some correlations are very high, while others are low or non-existent.

8.3   Negative correlations

So far we have been talking about the amount of *positive* correlation between pairs of scores. In Table 8.1 arithmetic scores were highly correlated with reading scores. But what about cases when high scores on one variable might be expected to be associated with *low* scores on another variable? For instance, children who achieve excellent scores on a quiz about sports may score low on writing essays, and vice versa.

It is important to realize that, if high scores on one variable are associated with low scores on another variable, there is still a correlation, but it is in the *opposite* direction to a positive correlation. This is known as a **negative correlation** because the scores are moving in the *opposite direction* to each other.

Question 26 Which of the following are likely to be positive correlations or negative correlations?

(a) Temperatures in winter and size of electricity bills.

(b) Amount of rain and sale of umbrellas.

Table 8.2 shows a set of scores which indicate that there is a negative correlation between scores on a sports quiz and essay scores. Check for

Table 8.2 Sports quiz scores and essay writing scores

Child	Sports quiz scores	Essay scores
1	10	1
2	9	2
3	8	3
4	7	4
5	6	5

each child that, the higher their sports quiz scores, the lower their essay scores and, the lower their quiz scores, the higher their essay scores. This means that the variables of sports quiz scores and essay scores are *negatively* correlated.

? Question 27 In Table 8.2 which children differ most in their sports quiz and essay scores and which children have much the same scores?

8.4 Correlation coefficients

We have discussed positive and negative correlations and demonstrated that they can be high, low or non-existent. The next question is how to measure precisely the amount of correlation between two variables.

Correlations are measured in terms of **correlation coefficients** which indicate the *size* of the correlation between two variables. Correlation coefficients run from zero, i.e. no correlation, to 1 for a perfect positive correlation. In Table 8.1 there is a complete one-to-one relationship between the pairs of scores for spelling and reading scores. This represents a *perfect positive correlation coefficient* between the variables of spelling scores and reading scores.

Unfortunately, in psychological research it is hard to think of any scores which would be so perfectly correlated. Because of the infinite variability of human beings, there are sure to be some good spellers who are bad at reading. For this reason, most correlations between psychological variables are *not* perfectly correlated. A correlation coefficient of 1 represents a perfect positive correlation; a correlation coefficient of 0 represents no correlation at all. Most positive correlations fall somewhere between these two extremes.

Positive correlation coefficients are expressed as numbers between 0 and 1. The nearer a correlation coefficient is to 0 the lower the correlation. The nearer it is to 1 the higher the positive correlation.

? Question 28 (a) Which of the three correlation coefficients listed below expresses the lowest and the highest correlations? List them in order from lowest to highest.

(i) 0.5   (ii) 0   (iii) 0.9

(b) Which of these correlation coefficients is most likely to express the relationship between number of miles travelled and the cost of a single second class ticket?

(c) Which of the correlational coefficients is most likely to express the relationship between the number of pedestrian crossings in a town and average earnings?

Negative correlation coefficients are also expressed as numbers, but this time between 0 and *minus* 1. Once again, the nearer a negative correlation coefficient is to 0 the lower the correlation. The nearer it is to −1 the higher the correlation.

To sum up, a correlation coefficient of zero means that there is no relation at all between the variables. A high negative correlation coefficient (say, −0.9) represents a large negative correlation, just as a high positive correlation coefficient (say, +0.9) represents a large positive correlation. It is a general rule that the higher the correlation coefficient, whether positive or negative, the higher the correlation. Smaller correlation coefficients (such as 0.2 and −0.2) indicate lower correlations between variables. Figure 8.2 shows the full range of possible correlation coefficients. (Note that it is a convention to drop the plus sign for positive correlations but to retain the minus sign to indicate a negative correlation.)

? Question 29 Which of the following coefficients represents the highest correlation?

+0.5   +1.1   0   −0.65

8.5 Testing the significance of correlations

As with all statistical tests, a correlational test gives the percentage probability that the scores in your experiment are due to random variability, as

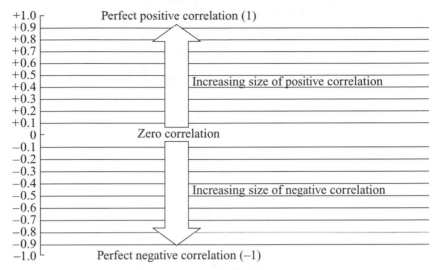

Figure 8.2 Range of correlation coefficients

stated by the null hypothesis. On the basis of the percentage probability of a random result, you can decide whether this probability is sufficiently low to reject the null hypothesis at $p < 0.05$ or $p < 0.01$, and instead to accept that there is a significant correlation in the predicted direction.

It is possible to make either a one-tailed or a two-tailed hypothesis about a correlation. A one-tailed hypothesis predicts a correlation in one direction: either a positive correlation is predicted or a negative correlation is predicted. A two-tailed hypothesis predicts that there will be some correlation between two variables but that it might go in either direction, e.g. that reading scores are likely to be associated either with high or with low arithmetic scores.

If you find any of these comments puzzling, reread Chapter 3, Sections 3.3 and 3.4.

If you look at Decision Chart 1 inside the *front cover* for non-parametric tests you will notice that at the top left-hand side there is a diamond which asks whether you are testing 'Correlations between scores?' If the answer is 'yes', the Spearman rank correlation coefficient will be the appropriate statistical test.

It is called a *rank* test because, as with the previous non-parametric tests, you will be ranking scores. It is called a rank 'correlation coefficient' test because it will work out a correlation coefficient ranging in size from 0 to 1, which represents the size of correlation in your data. So an experimenter might report a positive correlation of 0.6 between two variables at a significance level of $p < 0.05$, meaning that there is a less than 5 per cent probability that the correlation was due to a random distribution of scores.

It is important to note that a correlation has to be high to be considered as possibly significant. If a researcher is investigating a very large number of subjects, a quite low correlation might turn out to be significant. However, unless there is a reasonably high correlation in the first place, the correlation may be significant but actually quite low. It is, therefore, a requirement to obtain a reasonably *high* correlation, say 0.6 or better, before carrying out a test to assess its significance.

 Progress box six

Positive and negative correlations

- Correlations represent the amount of *association* between scores on two variables.
- Correlations are measured on a scale running from +1 (perfect *positive* correlation) through 0 (no correlation) down to −1 (perfect *negative* correlation).
- It is good practice to require a reasonably *high correlation* before looking up its significance.
- Having looked up the *percentage probability* of obtaining an observed size of correlation, you can decide whether the probability of a random result is low enough ($p < 0.05$ or $p < 0.01$) for you to reject the null hypothesis and accept that there is a significant correlation as predicted by the experimental hypothesis.

8.6   Spearman rank correlation coefficient

When to use

This is a non-parametric test which measures the significance of a *correlation* between people's scores on *two* variables.

Sample data

We will use as sample data the arithmetic and reading scores for 12 children shown in Table 8.3. Note that the same two variables are being studied as in Table 8.1. But this time the data are more realistic, with some children scoring more highly on arithmetic than reading and vice versa.

Table 8.3   Arithmetic scores (out of 10) and reading scores (out of 5)

Child	Spelling scores	Reading scores
1	5	2
2	3	2
3	7	4
4	10	5
5	9	4
6	9	5
7	2	4
8	6	3
9	3	1
10	4	1
11	8	4
12	10	5

Hypothesis

The prediction is that high arithmetic scores will be positively correlated with high reading scores. This is a one-tailed hypothesis predicting a correlation in one direction.

Rationale

The Spearman test calculates a statistic called *rho* (denoted r_S) which measures the correlation coefficient between two sets of scores. If two variables are predicted to be positively correlated, subjects who have low ranks on one of them should also have low ranks on the other and subjects who are ranked highly on one should also be ranked highly on the other. However, if there is no correlation (i.e. a random distribution of ranks as stated by the null hypothesis) the two sets of ranks will not be related.

Preparing the data

The Spearman test is based on allocating ranks. Table 8.4 shows the arithmetic scores and reading scores given in Table 8.3. Each set of scores is ranked *separately* and it is the *differences between ranks* (not scores) which are calculated in the *d* column. Reading ranks have been subtracted from spelling ranks. You probably found it quite difficult to work out the ranks for all the tied scores, especially for the reading scores. This is always a problem when the range of scores on a variable is limited (scores out of 10 or 5).

Table 8.4 Correlation between arithmetic and reading scores (Spearman)

Subjects (N)	Arithmetic scores	Arithmetic ranks (A)	Reading scores	Reading ranks (B)	d	d^2
1	5	5	2	3.5	+1.5	2.25
2	3	2.5	2	3.5	−1	1
3	7	7	4	7.5	−0.5	0.25
4	10	11.5	5	11	+0.5	0.25
5	9	9.5	4	7.5	+2	4
6	9	9.5	5	11	−1.5	2.25
7	2	1	4	7.5	−6.5	42.25
8	6	6	3	5	+1	1
9	3	2.5	1	1.5	+1	1
10	4	4	1	1.5	+2.5	6.25
11	8	8	4	7.5	+0.5	0.25
12	10	11.5	5	11	+0.5	0.25
						$\Sigma d^2 = 61$

Look back to Chapter 5 to refresh your memory about how to rank scores.

Step-by-step instructions for calculating r_s

If you look at the formula in Box G you will see that the final step is to subtract from 1 at the end of the calculation. You will remember that +1 represents a perfect positive correlation. The *smaller* the number you subtract from 1, the *higher* the positive correlation. In Box G, the last step is $1 - 0.21$, giving the relatively high positive correlation of 0.79.

Looking up the significance of r_s in Table H

Along the top row of the table you will find various levels of significance for one-tailed and two-tailed tests. The value of r_s has to be *equal to* or *larger than* the values in Table H to be significant. In the left-hand column you will find N (number of subjects); in our example $N = 12$. The calculated r_s of 0.79 exceeds the critical value of 0.777 for $p < 0.005$ (one-tailed) and it can therefore be concluded that there is a significant relationship between the two variables. (Note that some values of N (number of subjects) are missing from Table H. If your N is one of these you should take the next smallest N, e.g. if you had 11 subjects you should look up the row for $N = 10$.)

■ **Box G**

Step-by-step instructions for calculating the value of r_s

1   Rank the arithmetic scores.   Arithmetic ranks (A) column in Table 8.4.

     Rank the reading scores.   Reading ranks (B) column in Table 8.4.

2   Calculate the difference (d) between each pair of A and B *ranks* by subtracting each rank B from each rank A.   See d column.

3   Square each difference in the d column. (Note that squaring a minus number results in a positive number.)   See d^2 column.

4   Add up the squares in the d^2 column to obtain Σd^2. $\Sigma d^2 = 61$

5   Note the number of subjects (N). $N = 12$

6   Calculate the value of r_s using the formula:

$$r_s = 1 - \frac{6\Sigma d^2}{N(N^2 - 1)}$$

$$r_0 = 1 - \frac{6 \times 61}{12(144 - 1)}$$

$$= 1 - \frac{366}{12 \times 143}$$

$$= 1 - \frac{366}{1716}$$

$$= 1 - 0.21$$

$$= 0.79$$

We have not yet said whether the correlation is significant in the predicted direction. As we obtained a *positive* value of r_s we can assume that this means that there is a *positive* correlation between spelling and reading. But remember that it is important to check there is a high correlation as well as calculating significance.

You would look up significance levels in Table H for a *negative correlation* in exactly the same way as for a positive r_s, because the probabilities in Table H are concerned with the *size* of a correlation, regardless of whether it has a positive or negative sign.

Conclusion

The positive correlation of 0.79 is significant ($p < 0.005$), which supports the prediction that arithmetic and reading scores are highly correlated.

? Question 30 (a) Look back to the sports quiz and essay scores in Table 8.2. Following the step-by-step instructions, calculate r_s and test its significance.
Note that any number multiplied by zero is zero; so the square of 0 is 0.
Is there anything special about this correlation?

(b) The scores shown in Table 8.5 were obtained from a test for memory of shapes and a test for spelling ability. Both tests were given to the same set of ten subjects.

Table 8.5 Shape memory scores and spelling scores

Subject	Shape memory	Ranks A	Spelling	Ranks B	d	d^2
1	7		13			
2	8		19			
3	6		16			
4	9		21			
5	4		10			
6	3		11			
7	9		18			
8	8		18			
9	10		14			
10	11		16			
						$\Sigma d^2 =$

(i) Use the blank columns to calculate the value of r_s.

(ii) Can the experimental hypothesis that shape memory is associated with spelling ability be accepted?

9 Chi-square test

9.1 Introduction

The chi-square test is totally different from all the other non-parametric tests in this book. Note that 'chi-square' can be written χ^2 and is pronounced 'ky-square'. The chi-square test is a suitable test to use only when subjects are assigned to one or more *categories*. Because each subject can be assigned to only one category, the chi-square test is only appropriate for making predictions about how many different subjects will fall into each category.

The essential characteristic of the chi-square test is that it does not deal with scores. Instead it should only be used for the *all-or-none behaviour* of subjects. One example would be if it were only possible to observe that people could solve a problem or not solve a problem. People could be put into the categories of solving or not solving the problem.

? Question 31 Suppose an experiment was carried out to discover whether giving subjects a hint would help them to solve a problem. The experimenter gave a hint to one group of subjects and no hint to another group of subjects.

(a) One experimenter measured the time taken by the two groups of subjects to solve the problem. What would be the appropriate test for this?

(b) Another experimenter measured which subjects in each group would solve or not solve the problem. Which would be the appropriate test for this?

A further point must be taken into consideration when using the chi-square test. In other experimental designs the experimenter decides how many subjects to have in each condition and so the number of scores in each group is predetermined. However, for the chi-square test the dependent variable measures how many subjects in each group will fall into certain categories; so this cannot be decided in advance. Consequently, you have to test quite a lot of subjects to make sure that a sufficient number turn out to be allocated to each category. The minimum is usually considered to be at least 20 subjects. This may sound rather a lot, but it does not usually take too long to carry out an experiment in which you are only going to count the number of subjects who fall into one category or another.

In Decision Chart 1 inside the *front cover* you will see at the top on the right-hand side a diamond asking whether the researcher is 'Counting categories'? This refers to counting how many people fall into one category or another and so the chi-square is the only appropriate test.

9.2   Chi-square test

When to use

When subjects are *allocated to categories*, the chi-square test should be used. Remember that it only deals with categories, *not* scores.

Sample data

Suppose a researcher wants to find out whether social science students employ a method of study which is significantly different from that used by technology students. Two groups are selected, one group of 50 social science students and one group of 50 technology students. A questionnaire is sent to all 100 students asking them to indicate whether their study method falls into one of three study patterns: regular day-to-day study, irregular concentrated bursts of intensive work or a mixture of both. There are 44 replies from social science students and 42 replies from technology students. These replies are allocated into one or other of three categories, regular, irregular or mixed study.

All chi-square test results are shown in the form of a table known as a **contingency table**. The 'cells' in the table represent each of the categories. Because there are two rows (social science and technology students) and three columns for the three types of study, the six cells are numbered 1 to 6 in Table 9.1. Remember that the numbers in each cell represent

Table 9.1 Contingency table of reported study patterns (observed frequencies)

	Study patterns			Totals of students
	Regular	*Irregular*	*Mixed*	
Group 1 (social science students)	Cell 1 6	Cell 2 15	Cell 3 23	44
Group 2 (technology students)	Cell 4 10	Cell 5 8	Cell 6 24	42
Totals for study patterns	16	23	47	86 Total number of subjects (*N*)

the *number of subjects* who fall into each category; they are *not* scores obtained from subjects (as was the case in all the previous tests described in this book). For instance, the 6 in cell 1 represents the six social science students who used regular study patterns. In Table 9.1 the totals have also been calculated for the cells. The 6 in cell 1 and the 10 in cell 4 add up to the total of 16. This represents the total of all students using regular study patterns.

? Question 32 (a) What do the 15 in cell 2 and the 23 in cell 3 represent?

(b) How many technology students reported:

(i) regular study patterns?

(ii) irregular study patterns?

(iii) mixed study patterns?

Hypothesis

The researcher predicted that a higher proportion of technology students would have regular study patterns than would social science students.

Rationale

The number of students in each cell can be thought of as *frequencies*. This is because the number in each cell represents the *frequency* with which social science or technology students fall into each study pattern category.

What the chi-square test does is to compare the **observed frequencies** in each of the squares (cells) of a contingency table with the **expected frequencies** for each cell. The test compares the frequency of actual numbers of students who fall into each cell as against the numbers of students we would expect to fall into each cell if there were in fact only random differences between the reported study patterns of the two types of students. We already know the *observed frequencies* resulting from our experiment (as shown in Table 9.1). But we have to estimate the *expected frequencies* derived from the numbers of each type of student and the distribution of study patterns.

Overall, there are 44 social science students and 42 technology students. But, in order to calculate the expected frequencies, we also have to consider the total number of students who report each of the study patterns. For instance, we have to take into account the fact that only 16 students out of a grand total of 86 students reported regular study patterns when calculating expected frequencies for this study pattern. We can work out the proportions of the 44 social science students and the 42 technology students who would be expected to report regular study patterns even if there were no real differences between the types of students. Similarly, expected frequencies can be calculated for the other cells on the basis of the overall number of students reporting irregular (23) and mixed (47) study patterns.

The first step is to identify the relevant marginal totals for cell 1. The number in cell 1 represents the observed number of 6 social science students who reported regular study patterns. To calculate the expected frequencies, the relevant marginal totals are those which indicate the total number of regular study patterns (16) and the total number of social science students (44). Given these marginal totals, it is possible to calculate the expected frequency of students in cell 1 if there were no bias in favour of social science students reporting one study pattern rather than another. In other words, the expected frequency for cell 1 represents the number of social science students who would be expected to report regular study patterns if the marginal totals of students are randomly distributed between cells. Using the same method it is possible to calculate the expected frequency for each individual cell from the marginal totals which are relevant to that cell (i.e. 16 and 44 for cell 1; 16 and 42 for cell 4, and so on).

The expected frequencies calculated from the marginal totals are then compared with the *actual* observed frequencies of students in each cell. In this way, it is possible to check whether there are more or fewer students in each cell than would be expected on the basis of random variability.

? Question 33 From Table 9.1 list the two relevant marginal totals for each of the following cells (giving the marginal totals for the study patterns first).

(a) Cell 1   (c) Cell 3   (e) Cell 5

(b) Cell 2   (d) Cell 4   (f) Cell 6

If the observed results are random they should approximate closely to the expected frequencies. But, if the observed frequencies in the cells differ significantly from the expected frequencies, then the experimental hypothesis will be supported.

On the question of appropriate number of subjects, the calculated expected frequencies should ideally come out to a minimum of 5 for each cell. This applies particularly when you only have two groups allocated to two categories, giving only four cells. When you have six cells, as in the 2×3 table shown in Table 9.1, you can still use the test if the number of expected frequencies in just one of the cells is under 5. Note that this requirement applies only to the *expected* frequencies. It does not matter how many of the observed frequencies are less than 5, i.e. the numbers of actual subjects who fall into each category.

Step-by-step instructions for calculating the value of χ^2

These are given in Box H. *N.B.* You will have to take the calculation of degrees of freedom (*df*) on trust here. You will be given full details about degrees of freedom in Chapter 11.

Box H

Step-by-step instructions for calculating the value of χ^2

1   Note the *observed frequencies* (O) in cells 1–6 in Table 9.1.

Cell 1: $O = 6$
Cell 2: $O = 15$
Cell 3: $O = 23$
Cell 4: $O = 10$
Cell 5: $O = 8$
Cell 6: $O = 24$

2   Calculate the *expected frequencies* (E) for cells 1–6 in Table 9.1 by multiplying the two relevant marginal totals for each cell and dividing by the total number of subjects N.

Cell 1: $E = \dfrac{16 \times 44}{86} = 8.19$

Cell 2: $E = \dfrac{23 \times 44}{86} = 11.77$

Cell 3: $E = \dfrac{47 \times 44}{86} = 24.05$

Cell 4: $E = \dfrac{16 \times 42}{86} = 7.81$

Cell 5: $E = \dfrac{23 \times 42}{86} = 11.23$

Cell 6: $E = \dfrac{47 \times 42}{86} = 22.95$

3   Calculate the value of χ^2 using the formula

$$\chi^2 = \sum \frac{(O - E)^2}{E}$$

Remember that squares of minus numbers result in positive numbers.

$$= \frac{(6 - 8.19)^2}{8.19} + \frac{(15 - 11.77)^2}{11.77} + \frac{(23 - 24.05)^2}{24.05}$$

$$+ \frac{(10 - 7.81)^2}{7.81} + \frac{(8 - 11.23)^2}{11.23} + \frac{(24 - 22.95)^2}{22.95}$$

$$= \frac{(-2.19)^2}{8.19} + \frac{(3.23)^2}{11.77} + \frac{(-1.05)^2}{24.05}$$

$$+ \frac{(2.19)^2}{7.81} + \frac{(-3.23)^2}{11.23} + \frac{(1.05)^2}{22.95}$$

$$= 0.58 \text{ (cell 1)} + 0.89 \text{ (cell 2)} + 0.05 \text{ (cell 3)}$$
$$+ 0.61 \text{ (cell 4)} + 0.93 \text{ (cell 5)} + 0.05 \text{ (cell 6)}$$
$$= 3.11$$

4   Calculate the degrees of
     freedom:
     c = number of columns $c = 3$
     r = number of rows $r = 2$
     $df = (c - 1)(r - 1)$ $df = (3 - 1) \times (2 - 1) = 2$

Looking up the significance of χ^2 in Table F

The statistic χ^2 reflects the size of the difference between observed and expected frequencies. The greater the difference between observed and expected frequencies, the more likely the result is to be significant; so the calculated value of χ^2 should be *equal to* or *larger than* the critical values given in Table F.

Table F gives critical values against which the calculated value of χ^2 can be compared. The level of significance depends on the degrees of freedom (df). In our example, $df = 2$ so you should look along that row. The calculated value of χ^2 is 3.11, which is less than the value of 5.99 for $p < 0.05$. Therefore, the results of our experiment are not significant. We cannot reject the null hypothesis that any differences between the study patterns of social science and technology students are due to random variability.

It is not possible to make a one-tailed prediction about the direction of results for a chi-square. A significant chi-square would indicate that there are overall differences between the observed frequencies of social science and technology students who fall into each of the study pattern categories. However, it is a good idea to insert the calculated E values for each cell (see step 2 of the step-by-step instructions) as is shown in Table 9.2. The difference between the observed frequency (O) and the expected frequency (E) for any particular cell indicates the extent to which an actual observed frequency departs from what would be expected according to the null hypothesis. So cells which show the biggest differences are those which have contributed most to any overall significant differences. For instance, in Table 9.2 cells 2 and 5 show the biggest differences between O and E. As predicted, there are more social sciences students and fewer technology students who report irregular study patterns than would be expected (i.e. in cell 2 an actual observed frequency of 15 against an expected frequency of 11.77; and in cell 5 an actual observed frequency of 8 against an expected frequency of 11.23). However, these are *not* significant differences because overall the calculated value of chi-square was not significant.

A final reminder about using Table F is to check first that the *expected* frequencies for each cell are 5 or more. The calculated expected frequencies

Table 9.2 Comparison between observed and expected frequencies (chi-square)

	Study patterns			*Marginal totals of students*
	Regular	*Irregular*	*Mixed*	
Group 1 (social science students)	1 6 E = 8.19	2 15 E = 11.77	3 23 E = 24.05	44
Group 2 (technology students)	4 10 E = 7.81	5 8 E = 11.23	6 24 E = 22.95	42
Marginal totals of study patterns	16	23	47	86 Grand total (N)

in our example are all above 5. You could still have gone ahead if the expected frequency in one cell had been under 5. But, if you find yourself with too many cells with expected frequencies under 5, you will have to use a different table of significance levels (known as the Fisher exact probability test) which you can find in a book by Siegel (1956). However, if you have about 20 subjects, and there is no reason to expect that the random probabilities for each cell are likely to be odd in any way, you should be able to use the chi-square test.

Conclusions

The overall pattern of differences between expected and observed frequencies showed no significant differences so the null hypothesis cannot be rejected that students' reported study patterns represent a random distribution.

? Question 34 In an experiment designed to investigate the effects of giving information about the advantages and disadvantages of helping other people, subjects were divided into two groups. The subjects in group 1 were given information about the advantages of helping other people, while the subjects in group 2 were told about the possible risks arising from trying to help people. The researcher then presented all the subjects with an opportunity to help an elderly person across a busy road. The measure was whether subjects helped or not; that is, whether they fell into the categories of helpers or non-helpers. The hypothesis was that the subjects in group 1, who had been given positive information in favour of helping, would act more helpfully. Table 9.3 shows the results in the form of a 2×2 contingency table.

Table 9.3   Number of helping responses

	Helped	*Did not help*	*Marginal totals*
Group 1 (advantages)	9	6	
Group 2 (risks)	3	12	
Marginal totals			*(N)*

(a) What was the independent variable? What was the dependent variable?

(b) How many subjects were there in group 1 and group 2? How many subjects in each group displayed helping behaviour?

(c) Calculate χ^2 following the step-by-step instructions in Box H.

(d) Is the experimental hypothesis one-tailed or two-tailed? What implications does this have for looking up the significance of χ^2 in Table F? Are the results of the experiment significant?

Part III Parametric tests

10 Requirements for parametric tests

10.1 Proportions of variability

With parametric tests it is possible to calculate proportions of total variability in scores which are due, on the one hand, to independent variables manipulated by the experimenter and, on the other, to irrelevant variables affecting subjects' performance.

The notion that total variability can be apportioned between different sources of variability is central to the use of parametric tests. As was pointed out in Chapter 1, life for psychological researchers would be simple if all the total variability in scores could be attributed to differences between experimental conditions as predicted by the experimental hypothesis. Unfortunately, human behaviour being what it is, there are always lots of unknown variables which are also producing differences in subjects' scores, such as individuals' abilities and motivations, different interpretations of the experimental task and so on. If these unpredictable sources of variability are large they may mask any predicted differences in scores due to manipulation of the independent variables.

Naturally, a researcher hopes that a *large* proportion of total variability in scores will be due to intended independent variables while a relatively *small* proportion will be due to other irrelevant variables. These proportions can be expressed as a *ratio*:

$$\frac{predicted\ variability\ due\ to\ independent\ variables}{total\ variability\ due\ to\ all\ variables}$$

The higher this ratio, the greater the proportion of total variability is due to the independent variables and the less due to unknown variables. What we need to know is how high this ratio of predicted variability must be to allow us to say that our experimental results are significant, rather than due to unpredictable random variability, as stated by the null hypothesis.

Parametric statistical tables give the probabilities of obtaining a high proportion of predicted variability in comparison with the amount of random variability. If the proportion of predicted variability is high, the predicted differences are likely to be significant. Another way of expressing this is that, if the percentage probability of random variability is low ($p < 0.05$ or $p < 0.01$), the null hypothesis can be rejected and the results of the experiment can be interpreted as supporting the predictions made by the experimental hypothesis.

Parametric tests are based on the ability to calculate the exact amount of variability in subjects' scores. The normal term used in parametric tests is **variance**. Variances represent calculated estimates of variability. So proportions of variability can be reformulated in terms of predicted variance and total variance:

$$\frac{predicted\ variance\ due\ to\ independent\ variables}{total\ variance\ due\ to\ all\ variables}$$

In order to carry out the precise mathematical calculations necessary to calculate variances, the scores which provide the data of the experiment have to be in a form which conforms to certain mathematical functions. These functions are known as *parameters*, hence the name parametric tests.

You may want to note here that non-parametric tests are called *non-parametric* because the data do not have to conform to the parameters described below. This is because for non-parametric tests the scores are ranked rather than calculated directly.

The requirements for the types of scores suitable for parametric tests are threefold. The way of measuring scores has to be suitable for numerical calculations of variance. The other two requirements are concerned with the distributions of scores. We will discuss each of these in turn.

10.2   Types of measurement

It is obviously a crucial matter to decide how you are going to measure the behaviour of your subjects. Having varied an independent variable, you have to obtain some measure of the dependent variable, e.g. improvement in reading scores or number of words recalled from a text. It is generally considered essential for the measurement of the dependent variable to be *objective* in the sense that the measure will always give the same results regardless of who is doing the measuring. This insistence on **objective measurement** does not necessarily mean that only rather uninteresting aspects of human behaviour can be studied. An objective measure might be people's responses to a questionnaire about their innermost feelings.

Table 10.1 Scores and ranks

	Condition 1		Condition 2	
	Scores	*Ranks*	*Scores*	*Ranks*
	10	7	180	7
	8	6	120	6
	7	5	108	5
	6	4	8	4
	5	3	2	3
	3	1.5	1	1.5
	3	1.5	1	1.5
Rank totals		28		28
Means	6		60	

The simplest type of measurement was introduced in Chapter 9. Chi-square should only be used when subjects can be allocated to *different categories*. This type of measurement is called **nominal measurement** because it can only give a label, or *name*, to the categories. The term nominal is derived from the word *name*.

Scores which can be ranked give rise to what is known as **ordinal measurement**. Ordinal measurement means that scores can be graded in the *order* of being larger or smaller. If scores cannot be ordered from smallest to biggest it would not be possible to allocate ranks, giving the lowest ranks to the smallest scores and the highest ranks to the highest scores. For non-parametric tests it was sufficient to rank scores. For instance, look at the scores shown in Table 10.1. These show the results of two conditions. As you can see, the ranks range from 1 to 7 and the rank totals are exactly the same for the scores in both experiments. But it is obvious that the means are quite different. Even more strikingly the amount of variability is quite different. Compare the small range of scores in condition 1 with the much wider range of scores in condition 2. The scores in Table 10.1 show quite clearly that all that matters is that scores can be ranked in *order* from smallest to biggest; it does not matter how big or small the differences between scores as long as they can be placed in order, hence *ordinal measurement*.

Finally, we come to a type of measurement which can result in *numerical* scores, such as numbers of items recalled or reading times. This type of measurement is known as **interval measurement** because it assumes *equal intervals* between scores on a continuous numerical scale. It is assumed that remembering two items as opposed to three items represents the same interval as that between remembering three and four items. Consequently, it is possible to perform numerical operations on this kind of data, in order to carry out the more complex kinds of statistical analysis required for parametric tests. Interval measurement means that scores can be added, subtracted, multiplied and divided.

So the first requirement for parametric tests is that the data from an experiment must be measured on at least an *interval scale*. This means that parametric tests should only be used when the scores are measured on a *continuous scale* of numerical data. Examples would be a continuous scale of reading times or numbers of items correctly recalled.

 Progress box seven

Types of measurement

Three types of measure are contrasted:
- Nominal: subjects are allocated to named categories.
- Ordinal: scores can be put in rank order from smallest to biggest.
- Interval: scores are on a continuous scale with equal intervals and can be used for numerical operations.

? **Question 35** Which types of measurement would be suitable for measuring:

(a) Pass or failure at an exam?

(b) Teachers' ratings of educational aptitude?

(c) Children's scores on an arithmetic test running from 0 to 100 per cent.

10.3   Normal distributions

A second requirement for parametric tests is that scores should be *normally distributed*. Look back to the histogram of recall scores in Figure 3.1 in Chapter 3, Section 1. One point you will notice about such a distribution of scores is that there tend to be more scores in the middle range than at either end of the histogram. This is a very general characteristic of distributions of scores. Think about the heights of the adult population. You would expect to find more people in the middle range of heights (say 5–6 ft) than adults who are extremely tall (6–7 ft) or extremely short (3–4 ft).

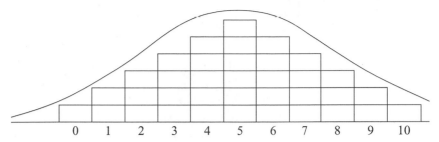

Figure 10.1   Normal distribution

Another characteristic feature of many distributions is that they are *symmetrical*. This means that there are equal numbers of scores on either side of the midpoint and that they fall off in a regular fashion to the left and right. Actually, the scores in the histogram in Figure 3.1 in Chapter 3, Section 1, are not distributed quite symmetrically because there is a tendency for there to be a greater bunching up of scores on the left-hand side. But imagine a completely symmetrical distribution of scores, as shown in Figure 10.1. This time there are exactly equal numbers of scores arranged in a symmetrical pattern on either side of the midpoint.

What the curved line in Figure 10.1 shows is a theoretical **normal distribution** for an infinite number of scores. However, it is important to realize that the continuous curve represents frequencies in exactly the same way as the squares in a histogram. With a histogram you can count up the exact frequencies of a finite number of scores. Since each square represents a score, the number of squares (i.e. the height of each column) tells you the frequency with which that score occurred. In exactly the same way the height of the distribution curve shows the frequencies of an infinite number of scores. The fact that the curve is tallest in the middle represents the fact that more scores are likely to occur in the middle range of scores while there are likely to be fewer extreme scores at the ends, or *tails*, of the distribution.

What you need to know is whether the scores in your experiment are *near enough* to being normally distributed to allow you to use parametric tests. One way of doing a rough check is to plot a distribution of all your scores in exactly the same way as was done in the histogram for the recall scores in Figure 3.1. All you need to do is to plot the values of the possible scores in your experiment along the bottom and allot a square every time one of your subjects gets that score. You can then see at a glance whether your total distribution of scores are roughly symmetrical around the midpoint. Because parametric tests are fairly 'robust', even when their assumptions are broken, you can go ahead with a parametric test unless your distribution of scores is very different from a normal distribution. Otherwise you would have to use a non-parametric test since these do not require interval measurement nor normal distributions.

A third formal requirement for parametric tests is termed **homogeneity of variance**. What this means is that the variability of the scores in each condition should be approximately the *same*. Look again at the scores for condition 1 and condition 2 in Table 10.1. It should be obvious that the range of variability in scores for these two conditions is noticeably different, the variability for condition 2 being much larger. The idea is that it would be difficult to make a comparison between the two conditions based on the numerical values of scores as different as these. One way of checking this is to plot separate histograms for each condition, as shown in Figure 3.2 in Chapter 3, Section 3.1.

Fortunately, such wide differences in the variability between two conditions are a rare occurrence. In any case, it has been shown that, as long as there are *equal* numbers of subjects in each condition, it does not matter too much whether the variability in scores in different conditions is completely homogeneous (i.e. the same). So this is another good reason for always allocating the *same number of subjects* to each experimental condition.

 Progress box eight

Requirements for parametric tests

- There are three requirements for parametric tests:

  (a) Experimental scores are measured on an *interval scale*.
  (b) Scores are *normally distributed*.
  (c) The variability of scores for each experimental condition should be roughly the same, i.e. *homogeneity of variance*.

- To test these assumptions it is essential that subjects' scores should be measured on a *numerical scale*. Plotting a histogram of all scores will give an indication of whether they have the roughly symmetrical shape of a normal distribution. Homogeneity of variance can be checked by plotting histograms for each condition but this is not so important as long as there are equal numbers of subjects in each experimental condition.
- Parametric tests are reasonably 'robust' as far as these criteria are concerned; unless your data are very divergent, you are unlikely to get seriously wrong answers about the percentage probabilities of obtaining the variance ratios in an experiment.
- If the experimental data do differ a lot from any of these three parametric assumptions, it may be safer to use an appropriate non-parametric test.

11 General method for parametric tests

11.1 Using Decision Chart 2

Decision Chart 2 inside the *back cover* includes the full range of statistical tests in this book. In the same way as for the simpler Decision Chart 1 inside the *front cover*, you should start by answering 'yes' to the diamond box 'Differences between conditions?' Work downwards answering the questions in each diamond box until you reach an oblong box showing appropriate statistics tests.

One big difference in Decision Chart 2 is that there is a diamond box which asks you whether you have selected an experiment which investigates 'One variable or two or more variables?' This is a crucial issue for selecting parametric tests. What happens if you select a one-variable design? This sends you to the *left-hand branch* of the decision chart. You will find that you have to answer the same questions as you did for the non-parametric tests: 'How many experimental conditions?' and 'Same or different subjects?'

When you have answered these questions you will be directed to oblong boxes which contain the non-parametric (non-para) tests you are familiar with and equivalent parametric (para) tests. This is because non-parametric tests and single-variable parametric tests are both suitable for analysing experiments which investigate only one variable at a time. So how does a researcher go about selecting a parametric or a non-parametric test?

11.2 Parametric versus non-parametric tests

Let us stress once again that the functions of both parametric and non-parametric statistical tests are exactly the same. In both cases an experimenter uses the tests to discover the probability that the results of an experiment occurred due to random fluctuations caused by unknown and irrelevant variables. On the basis of this the researcher can decide whether the probability of random variability is low enough to warrant rejecting the null hypothesis and accepting support for the experimental hypothesis.

The difference between parametric and non-parametric tests concerns the *method* of calculating these random probabilities. With non-parametric tests this is done by rank-ordering scores. If high or low ranks tend to occur in some conditions rather than others, this indicates that the scores are less likely to have occurred due to random variability but instead are due to predicted differences between experimental conditions.

It can be argued that the non-parametric method of *ordinal measurement*, placing scores into rank order, is measuring the variability in subjects' scores indirectly. Parametric tests, on the other hand, by taking advantage of *interval measurement*, can measure precise numerical proportions of total variability which are due to differences between experimental conditions. This makes parametric tests more 'powerful' in the sense that they take into account more information about differences in scores. Ranking scores only puts them in order of magnitude, whereas parametric tests calculate the numerical values of scores for calculating variances. Parametric tests should be more sensitive in picking up significant differences between subjects' performance in different experimental conditions.

If you find these references to ordinal measurement and interval measurement puzzling, turn back to Chapter 10, Section 10.2, to refresh your memory.

There has been a lot of argument about this question of the relative power of non-parametric and parametric tests among statisticians. Not all of them agree that parametric tests are that much more powerful than non-parametric tests. So on this basis alone there is no compelling reason against using the simpler non-parametric tests for analysing data. Deciding between parametric and non-parametric tests for dealing with a single independent variable, researchers have to weigh up the advantages of using a possibly more sensitive parametric test. Against this is the problem of trying to meet the requirements for applying parametric tests to experimental data.

Look back to Chapter 10 and Progress box eight to refresh your memory about the requirements for parametric tests.

To summarize, use a parametric test in the following conditions:

(a) the scores are numerical (interval scale);
(b) the scores approximate to a normal distribution;
(c) the variability in conditions does not differ too much.

If any of (a) to (c) are not applicable, it may be better to select a non-parametric test. One final point is that the calculations for parametric tests are more complicated because they calculate variances rather than ranks. But with the statistical computer packages now available this is not as great a problem as it used to be.

Progress box nine

Parametric and non-parametric tests

	Advantages	*Disadvantages*
Parametric tests	• They calculate numerical variances and therefore may be more sensitive to differences between conditions	• The experimental data have to meet the three requirements of interval measurement, normal distribution and homogeneity of variance
Non-parametric tests	• They can be used for investigating the effects of single variables when your experimental data do not meet the requirements for parametric tests	• Because non-parametric tests can only look at the effects of single variables in isolation, they ignore a lot of the complexity of human behaviour
	• They can be used to look at *trends* as well as overall differences between experimental conditions	• Because they make use of rank ordering rather than exact numerical calculations of variance, they are less likely to pick up significant differences
	• Most of the calculations are quick and easy	

11.3 Symbols used in parametric tests

It has been claimed that parametric tests can measure the precise numerical proportions of total variability. The basic method is to calculate the *squares* of numbers. This is why parametric tests require *interval measurement*. Another point to note is that when you calculate the squares of positive and minus scores you always end up with positive numbers.

Question 36 Calculate the squares of the following numbers. We have given the square of the first two numbers to start you off.

$$5 \times 5 = 25$$

$$(-5) \times (-5) = 25$$

10

−3

The next step is to add up individual squares to arrive at what is known as a *sum of squares*. In some of the step-by-step instructions for non-parametric tests the symbol Σ (pronounced *sigma*) was used for adding up totals of ranks. In parametric tests it is the squares of *scores* which are totalled. The symbol for a score is x and the symbol for a squared score is x^2. So Σx^2 means sum all the squared scores to arrive at a sum of squares. The same symbols apply to any squared numbers.

However, you will also come across another symbol $(\Sigma x)^2$. This may look similar to Σx^2 but it means that all the scores should first be totalled (Σx) and then the *total* of all scores should itself be squared $(\Sigma x)^2$. Here whatever is inside the brackets should be squared. Σx^2 has no brackets and so each *individual* score has to be first squared, and only then summed.

 Question 37 Suppose the scores in an experiment are 4, 5, 7, 8, 10.

(a) Calculate the value of Σx^2.

(b) Calculate the value of $(\Sigma x)^2$.

Remember, if you forget the meanings of any of these symbols, which are constantly used in all parametric tests, you can look back to this section.

11.4 Types of parametric tests

The main types of tests depend on whether there are two conditions or three or more conditions. For *two conditions* there are specially designed kinds of statistical analysis known as the *t* tests. These are designed to analyse *related designs* and *unrelated designs*.

Table 11.1 ANOVA sources of variance

Sources of variance	Proportions of variance
Independent variables (predicted)	Between-conditions variance
Irrelevant variables (unpredicted)	Error variance
Combination of independent and irrelevant variables	Total variance

The type of analysis suitable for *three or more* conditions has the general name of analysis of variance (often abbreviated as ANOVA). In the simplest kinds of ANOVA the sources of variance include: (i) variance due to the predicted independent variable; (ii) variance due to unknown random variables; and (iii) total variance due to variability in all scores. Because unpredictable variance is due to unknown uncontrollable irrelevant variables it is often called *error variance*.

Reread Chapter 10, Section 10.1, to refresh your memory about proportions of variability.

In ANOVA these three sources of variance are called:

(i) *between conditions* (predicted effects of independent variables);
(ii) *error variance* (unpredictable random variables);
(iii) *total variance* (all variability in data).

11.5 Degrees of freedom

There is one other important consideration which has to be taken into account when calculating variances and for looking up statistics in parametric statistics tables. The need for **degrees of freedom** arises from the very notion that parametric tests calculate variances based on variability in scores. It is essential therefore that all scores which are part of the calculations are 'free' to vary. The issue is whether all scores from an experiment are equally variable.

The concept of degrees of freedom is quite a difficult one to grasp. An example may help. Imagine that you are seating eight people round a table. When you have told seven people where to sit, this means that the eighth person must sit on the only chair left. There is no 'freedom' about where the last person will sit. So we would say that, although there are eight people (N), there are only seven degrees of freedom ($N - 1$). Convince yourself that this applies however many people you are trying to seat in the first place.

Now imagine that you are old-fashioned enough to be trying to seat four men and four women in alternate seats around the table. Once you have seated three men and three women, everyone would know where the last man and the last woman would have to sit. When there are two groups of four subjects, one person in each group has their place fixed for them and so is not 'free' to select their seat.

Now let us take an experimental example. Suppose you carry out an experiment and calculate the total of the scores. When copying out the scores later, you forget to include one of them, so that you end up with the scores shown in Table 11.2. You do not need to panic because you know that, given five scores and the total of all six scores, you can calculate the forgotten score. All you have to do is to subtract the five scores from the total; your sixth score could only have been 15. This means that the score for subject 6 is predictable from knowing the other scores and the total. So it has no 'freedom' to vary. There are therefore $6 - 1 = 5$ degrees of freedom.

Table 11.2 Degrees of freedom

S_1	12
S_2	13
S_3	10
S_4	11
S_5	14
S_6	–
Total	75

Question 38 Suppose there are four conditions in an experiment and that the total scores for each condition are as shown in Table 11.3.

Table 11.3 Calculating missing scores

	Total scores
Condition 1 (four subjects)	8
Condition 2 (four subjects)	12
Condition 3 (four subjects)	20
Condition 4 (four subjects)	–
All subjects ($N = 16$)	56

(a) Calculate the total score for condition 4.

(b) How many degrees of freedom are there for conditions?

(c) How many degrees of freedom are there for *N*?

The point about the examples in Question 38 is that, given the other scores and the total, the missing score is completely predictable, in other words it cannot *vary*. It is just because of this 'lack of freedom' for one score to vary that degrees of freedom (*df*) are calculated on the basis of scores that *can* vary, that is, $N - 1$ or $C - 1$. Since parametric statistical texts are based on distributions of variability, degrees of freedom to vary will need to be taken into account when looking up statistical probabilities.

The rules for calculating degrees of freedom are somewhat more complicated for ANOVA designs because it is necessary to compute degrees of freedom (*df*) for each source of variance. The rules for calculating (*df*) for ANOVA are shown in Progress box ten.

 Progress box ten

Degrees of freedom for ANOVA

We need three rules for calculating degrees of freedom (*df*) for ANOVA:

1 The *df* for each independent variable *between conditions* is calculated by subtracting one from the number of conditions used to test that variable ($C - 1$).

2 The *df* for the *total variance* is calculated by subtracting one from the total number of scores produced by all the subjects ($N - 1$).

3 The *df* for the *error variance* is calculated by subtracting the *df* for independent variables from the total *df*. It is for this reason that error is sometimes known as **residual error**, i.e. what is 'left over' after all the other variances and *df* have been calculated.

You will need *df* for dividing the sums of squares to arrive at mean square variances; and also when you come to look up the significance of *F* ratios in the appropriate statistical table.

It may help to apply the rules in Progress box ten to a concrete example. Take an experiment with *three* conditions and *six* different subjects in each condition, a total of 18 subjects:

Rule 1 df_{bet} Conditions minus 1: $C - 1 = 3 - 1 = 2$
Rule 2 df_{tot} Total number of subjects minus 1: $N - 1 = 18 - 1 = 17$
Rule 3 df_{error} $(N - 1)$ minus $(C - 1)$: $18 - 2 = 15$

You need not worry too much at this stage about this rather complex notion of degrees of freedom. You will be told exactly what to do whenever degrees of freedom come up in connection with a statistical test.

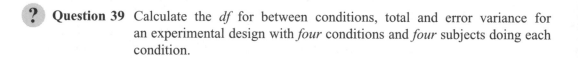

? Question 39 Calculate the *df* for between conditions, total and error variance for an experimental design with *four* conditions and *four* subjects doing each condition.

11.6   Looking up parametric statistical tables

There are many similarities between the non-parametric statistical tables you used in Part II and the parametric statistical tables you will be using in Part III. In both cases the tables provide calculated probabilities of obtaining experimental scores due to random variability. It is important, too, to know whether your experimental hypothesis is one-tailed or two-tailed.

Reread Chapter 3, Sections 3.3 and 3.4, to refresh your memory about levels of significance and one-tailed and two-tailed hypotheses.

You will remember that there were quite different statistical tables for each of the tests in Part II. This was because the different statisticians who had invented each test had done their own calculations of random probabilities. One piece of really good news is that all parametric tests calculate variances in a similar way. Because of this there are only two parametric tables: Table I for looking up the *t* test for two conditions, and Table J for all ANOVA tests. So, although the calculations of variance may be more onerous in the first place, there is no problem about how to look up statistic tables. Instead of having to make an adjustment for each table, the instructions for looking up parametric tests in statistical tables are uniform for all experimental designs. You will nevertheless be given precise instructions for each parametric statistical test.

11.7   Parametric tests, step by step

We will be presenting parametric tests in the order shown in Table 11.4. Note that for most parametric tests we will be giving you the tests for unrelated designs first because these are on the whole easier to calculate.

Table 11.4   Parametric tests

	Related designs *(same subjects)*	Unrelated designs *(different subjects)*
Chapter 12 Two conditions	*t* test (related)	*t* test (unrelated)
Chapter 13 Three or more conditions	One-way ANOVA (related)	One-way ANOVA (unrelated)
Chapter 15 Two-way ANOVA	Two-way ANOVA (related)	Two-way ANOVA (unrelated)
	Two-way ANOVA (mixed)	

This does *not* apply, however, to the very first test, the unrelated *t* test. We often tell students that this is the 'worst' calculation of all. If you can keep your head and work through the various parts of this formula in the correct order, all subsequent calculations will seem like child's play.

The *t* tests are differentiated from ANOVA for several reasons. First, they can only be used for testing differences between *two conditions* when only *one variable* is being manipulated, whereas ANOVA can be extended to cover cases when several conditions are used to test *two or more variables*. When we come to tackling ANOVA, we will start with one-way ANOVA (unrelated), which is the simplest of all. Two-way ANOVA (unrelated) is also much easier to grasp than two-way ANOVA (related).

The information given for each parametric test is divided into various sections.

1 *When to use*. This reminds you of appropriate experimental designs for which you can use the test.
2 *Sample data*. This gives a sample set of data which can be analysed using the test.
3 *Hypothesis*. This states the prediction that the experiment is designed to test.
4 For ANOVA tests, a *sources of variance table*. This includes the appropriate variances for the independent variables, error variance and total variance.
5 *Rationale*. In this section you will be told the rationale for using particular methods for calculating variances.
6 *Preparing the data*. The main type of calculation, with which you will soon become all too familiar, is to square a lot of numbers and then

add up these squares. As long as you have a pocket calculator with a cumulative memory $\boxed{M+}$ facility there is a simple method for doing this. Simply square each number and accumulate it in memory. Even more helpful would be to invest in a calculator which has a 'sums of squares' facility which does all the calculations automatically. We will also be introducing the use of computer packages for more complex parametric calculations. As with the calculations for the non-parametric tests, you may find that your answers differ from ours in the last decimal place, depending on whether intermediate figures have been rounded up. Obviously, such slight differences do not matter.

7 *Step-by-step instructions*. This section takes you through the calculations, giving formulae in the most convenient order for carrying out the calculations.

8 *Looking up significance in tables*. This section gives precise instructions about how to look up the significance of parametric tests in the appropriate statistical tables.

9 *Conclusions*. This section states the results of the experiment and whether they are significant.

12.1 t test (related)

When to use

The related t test is used for experimental designs with *two conditions* testing *one independent variable*, when the *same* subjects are doing both conditions (a *related design*). As you can see from Decision Chart 2 inside the back cover of the book, the related t test is the parametric equivalent of the non-parametric Wilcoxon test for *related designs* with *two experimental conditions*.

Sample data

Subjects were given 2 minutes to read a simple text and a complex text and were told that after 10 minutes they would be asked to recall the words. The same subjects were presented with both texts, half of the subjects with the simple text first and half with the complex text first. The results are shown in Table 12.1.

Hypothesis

The experimenter predicted that more words would be recalled from the simple text.

Rationale

The aim is to compare the predicted differences between the two experimental conditions against the total variability in the scores. When the

Table 12.1   Number of words recalled (related *t*)

Subjects	Condition 1 (simple text)	Condition 2 (complex text)	d	d^2
1	10	2	8	64
2	5	1	4	16
3	6	7	−1	1
4	3	4	−1	1
5	9	4	5	25
6	8	5	3	9
7	7	2	5	25
8	5	5	0	0
9	6	3	3	9
10	5	4	1	1
			$\Sigma d = 27$	$\Sigma d^2 = 151$
Means	6.4	3.7		

same subjects are used for both conditions, it is possible to compare pairs of scores obtained by each individual subject when performing under the two conditions. These differences in scores are compared against the total variance in the differences between all scores. If there are only random differences between the scores in the two conditions, as stated by the null hypothesis, the variance due to the predicted differences would be relatively small in relation to the total variability in scores.

Preparing the data

The scores for the *t* test (related) should be laid out as in Table 12.1 with the number for each subject on the left to show that the same subject did both experimental conditions. It is essential to calculate the means for the scores in each condition. Columns are added for calculating differences which, as with the Wilcoxon test in Chapter 6, are calculated by subtracting condition 2 scores from condition 1. This time the differences are not ranked. Instead each difference is squared and summed (see Σd^2). Note that the differences between the two conditions are treated as the variance due to predicted differences between conditions. The equation at the bottom of the formula calculates the total variance in scores due to all sources of variability.

  The calculations in Box I will be much easier if you invest in a calculator which has a sum of squares button ($\boxed{\Sigma x^2}$) which automatically works out squares and adds them up. But if you have a calculator with a memory at least you can put each square into memory and record the total sum of squares.

Box I

Step-by-step instructions for calculating *t* (related)

1 Calculate the differences between subjects' scores by subtracting condition 2 scores from condition 1.

See column *d* in Table 12.1.

2 Sum differences, taking into account pluses and minuses.

$\Sigma d = 27$

3 Square the differences.

See column d^2.

4 Sum the squared differences.

$\Sigma d^2 = 151$

5 Square the total of differences.

$(\Sigma d)^2 = 27 \times 27 = 729$

6 Total number of subjects

$N = 10$

7 Find *t* from the formula:

$$t = \frac{\Sigma d}{\sqrt{\dfrac{N\Sigma d^2 - (\Sigma d)^2}{N - 1}}}$$

$$t = \frac{27}{\sqrt{\dfrac{10 \times 151 - (27)^2}{10 - 1}}}$$

$$= \frac{27}{\sqrt{\dfrac{1510 - 729}{9}}}$$

$$= \frac{27}{\sqrt{86.78}}$$

$\sqrt{}$ = take the square root

$$= \frac{27}{9.315}$$

$$= 2.89$$

8 Calculate the degrees of freedom.

$df = N - 1 = 10 - 1 = 9$

Step-by-step instructions for calculating *t* (related)

These are given in Box I.

Looking up the significance of *t* in Table I

The statistic *t* calculates the ratio between predicted differences and total variability. The calculated value of *t* has to be *equal to* or *larger than* the values in Table I to be significant. In the step-by-step instructions you were asked to calculate the degrees of freedom, which were the total number of subjects (N) minus one. In order to look up the significance of t in Table I, look down the left-hand column and find the degrees of freedom (in our example 9). The hypothesis was one-tailed and the calculated t of 2.89 is larger than the critical value of 2.82 for $p < 0.01$.

Look back to Chapter 11, Section 11.5, to refresh your memory about degrees of freedom and why they are necessary when calculating variances for parametric tests.

Conclusions

Looking at the means in Table 12.1, the results are significant in the predicted direction, supporting the one-tailed hypothesis that more words are remembered from simple texts than from complex texts ($p < 0.01$).

? **Question 40** (a) Calculate the means of condition 1 and condition 2 in Table 12.2.

(b) Carry out a t test (related) on these scores following the step-by-step instructions, assuming that the scores came from the same subjects doing both conditions.

(c) What are the degrees of freedom (df)? Is t significant and, if so, at what level of significance for a one-tailed test? What conclusions can be drawn?

Table 12.2 Data for related t

Subjects	Condition 1	Condition 2	d	d^2
1	6	2		
2	7	1		
3	8	3		
4	10	4		
5	8	3		
6	8	2		
7	5	7		
8	3	4		
Means			Σd	Σd^2

12.2 *t* **test (unrelated)**

When to use

The unrelated *t* test is used for experimental designs with *two conditions* testing *one independent variable*, when different subjects are doing the *two conditions* (an *unrelated design*). The unrelated *t* test is the parametric equivalent of the non-parametric Mann–Whitney test for *unrelated designs* with *two experimental conditions*.

Sample data

Two groups of different subjects were used for each condition. One group were asked to read a simple text and the other group were given a complex text. Both groups were given 2 minutes to read the text and after 10 minutes were asked to recall as many words as they could. The results are shown in the Scores columns of Table 12.3.

Hypothesis

The experimenter predicted that more words would be recalled from the simple text.

Table 12.3 Number of words recalled (unrelated *t*)

	Condition 1 (simple text)		Condition 2 (complex text)	
	Scores (x_1)	Squared scores (x_1^2)	Scores (x_2)	Squared scores (x_2^2)
	10	100	2	4
	5	25	1	1
	6	36	7	49
	3	9	4	16
	9	81	4	16
	8	64	5	25
	7	49	2	4
	5	25	5	25
	6	36	3	9
	5	25	4	16
	Σx_1 64	Σx_1^2 450	Σx_2 37	Σx_2^2 165
Means	M_1 6.4		M_2 3.7	

Rationale

The aim is to compare the amount of variability due to the predicted differences in scores between the two conditions as against the total variability in subjects' scores. The predicted differences are calculated as a difference between the mean scores for the two groups. This difference between the means has to be compared against the total variance in all scores. If there are only random differences between the scores in the two conditions, as stated by the null hypothesis, the variance due to the predicted differences would be relatively small in relation to the total variability in scores.

Preparing the data

In the case of an unrelated design it is not possible to compare scores between individual subjects. The emphasis is on comparisons between the different groups of subjects doing each condition. In Table 12.3 each score is squared and summed for condition 1 and condition 2 separately ($\sum x_1^2$ and $\sum x_2^2$). The horrendous-looking formula given in step 6 of the step-by-step instructions shows the differences between the means for the two conditions on the top line. Below the line the separate variances for each condition are calculated, added together and divided by the combined degrees of freedom for each group of subjects. Finally, you have to take the square root of the total variance so that it can be directly compared against the absolute value of the difference between the means. All this will seem less formidable (we hope!) as you work your way through the formula.

It is possible to do these calculations on a calculator with a square root button and a memory store. But it would certainly be easier to use a more professional calculator which can automatically square numbers and sum squares.

Step-by-step instructions for calculating *t* (unrelated)

These are given in Box J.

Looking up the significance of *t* in Table I

The statistic *t* calculates the ratio between predicted differences and total variability. In order to be significant the calculated value of *t* has to be *equal to* or *larger than* the values in Table I. Because there are two groups of subjects a separate *df* is calculated for each group, the number of subjects in each group minus one, and these are then added together, $(n_1 - 1) + (n_2 - 1)$.

■ **Box J**

Step-by-step instructions for calculating *t* **(unrelated)**

1 Sum the totals of scores for each condition (see Table 12.3) and square these.

$(\Sigma x_1)^2 = 64 \times 64 = 4096$
$(\Sigma x_2)^2 = 37 \times 37 = 1369$

2 Calculate the means for each condition.

$M_1 = 6.4$
$M_2 = 3.7$

3 Square the individual scores for each condition.

See columns for squared scores in Table 12.3.

4 Sum the squared scores for each condition separately.

$\Sigma x_1^2 = 450$
$\Sigma x_2^2 = 165$

5 Number of subjects in each condition

$n_1 = 10$
$n_2 = 10$

6 Calculate the value of *t* using the formula

$$t = \frac{M_1 - M_2}{\sqrt{\dfrac{\left(\Sigma x_1^2 - \dfrac{(\Sigma x_1)^2}{n_1}\right) + \left(\Sigma x_2^2 - \dfrac{(\Sigma x_2)^2}{n_2}\right)}{(n_1 - 1) + (n_2 - 1)}\left(\dfrac{1}{n_1} + \dfrac{1}{n_2}\right)}}$$

$$t = \frac{6.4 - 3.7}{\sqrt{\dfrac{\left(450 - \dfrac{4096}{10}\right) + \left(165 - \dfrac{1369}{10}\right)}{9 + 9}\left(\dfrac{1}{10} + \dfrac{1}{10}\right)}}$$

$$= \frac{2.7}{\sqrt{\dfrac{(450 - 409.6) + (165 - 136.9)}{18} \times \dfrac{1}{5}}}$$

$$= \frac{2.7}{\sqrt{3.806 \times 0.2}}$$

$$= \frac{2.7}{\sqrt{0.7612}}$$

$$= 3.096$$

(*N.B.* It does not matter whether subtracting M_2 from M_1 results in a plus or minus number. When looking up the value of *t* simply ignore the sign)

7 Calculate the degrees of freedom by subtracting one from the number of subjects in each condition in turn and adding together the results.

$n_1 - 1 = 9$
$n_2 - 1 = 9$
$df = 9 + 9 = 18$

Because there are ten subjects in each condition $n_1 - 1 = 9$ and $n_2 - 1 = 9$. So for the combined *df* we have $9 + 9 = 18$. We look down the left-hand column of Table I to find 18 *df* and look along this row. The calculated *t* of 3.096 is larger than 2.878, indicating a significance level of $p < 0.005$ for a one-tailed hypothesis (or $p < 0.01$ for a two-tailed hypothesis).

Conclusions

Looking back to the means in Table 12.3, the results are significant in the predicted direction, supporting the one-tailed hypothesis that more words are remembered from simple texts ($p < 0.005$).

 Question 41 (a) Would it be more sensible to use same or different subjects for the sample experiment described in Sections 12.1 and 12.2?

(b) What are the similarities and differences between the Mann–Whitney and the unrelated *t*?

---

13 One-way ANOVA

13.1 Understanding ANOVA tables

ANOVA tables show all the formulae necessary to estimate different sources of variance. These tables contain many complicated-looking symbols, but we will be explaining each of these in turn (see Table 13.1). One important feature of all ANOVA tables is that all the sources of variance add up to the total variance. This makes it possible to work out the error variance by subtracting the between-conditions variance from the total variance. You will be pleased to hear that this is quite a shortcut which avoids having to calculate the error variance separately.

Calculating sums of squares

For each source of variance the first step is to calculate a **sum of squares (SS)** for each source of variance. The general method for calculating sums of squares is to square each score and add them up.

1 To estimate *total variance* all individual scores are squared and summed, which we write as $\sum x^2$.
2 To estimate *between-conditions variance* the totals for each condition are squared and summed, indicated by $\sum T^2$.
3 To estimate *error variance* subtract between-conditions variance from total variance.

Notice the difference between squaring each score and summing them, indicated by $\sum x^2$, and summing all the scores and then squaring that total, indicated by $(\sum x)^2$.

$(\sum x)^2$ divided by the number of all the scores (N) is known as a *constant* because it is subtracted from all SS in ANOVA calculations,

indicated by $\dfrac{(\sum x)^2}{N}$

Table 13.1   One-way ANOVA sources of variance table

Sources of variance	Sums of squares	Degrees of freedom	Mean squares	F ratios
Between conditions	SS_{bet}	df_{bet}	$\dfrac{SS_{bet}}{df_{bet}}$	$\dfrac{MS_{bet}}{MS_{error}}$
Error	SS_{error}	df_{error}	$\dfrac{SS_{error}}{df_{error}}$	
Total	SS_{tot}	df_{tot}		

Degrees of freedom

You were introduced to degrees of freedom (df) in Chapter 11, Section 11.5. These are needed in ANOVA calculations and for looking up ANOVA statistical tables.

Look back to Chapter 11, Section 11.5, and Progress box ten to refresh your memory about how to calculate degrees of freedom for ANOVA.

Mean squares and *F* ratios

Mean squares (*MS*) are calculated by dividing sums of squares (*SS*) by the appropriate degrees of freedom. It is these mean squares which are used to calculate *F ratios* (see the fourth column of Table 13.1). These are the ratios which represent comparisons between proportions of variance. In general, *F* ratios compare the amount of predicted variance between subjects due to the independent variable against the error variance which represents unpredictable, unknown variability. Thus, in the last column of Table 13.1, the between-conditions mean square (MS_{bet}) is divided by the error mean square (MS_{error}) to produce the *F* ratio.

F ratios represent the *statistic* which is looked up in ANOVA statistical tables. These tables give the probabilities of finding large or small *F* ratios. If the value of a *F* ratio is large enough to be significant at an accepted significance level, the experimenter can claim that significant differences between conditions support the hypothesis.

It may seem a long and complex business to calculate sums of squares (*SS*) and divide them by degrees of freedom (*df*) for each source of variance. But the point of the whole exercise is to calculate *F* ratios which can decide whether the results of an experiment are significant.

▶ **Progress box eleven**

ANOVA Tables

- Decide whether your experimental scores meet the *three parametric assumptions* listed in Progress box eight (Chapter 10).
- Draw up an ANOVA *sources of variance table*, showing the between-conditions variance, error variance and total variance.
- Calculate the *sums of squares* (*SS*), *degrees of freedom* (*df*) and *mean squares* (*MS*) for each source of variance.
- Calculate the *F ratio* by dividing MS_{bet} by MS_{error} and indicate the appropriate *df* for MS_{bet} and the *df* for MS_{error}
- Look up the *F ratios* in Table J to discover the probability that your results could be a random result due to error variance, as stated by the null hypothesis. If this probability is below 5 per cent or 1 per cent, reject the null hypothesis at the $p < 0.05$ or $p < 0.01$ significance level.

One-way ANOVA designs like that shown in Table 13.1 do not require very difficult calculations. The main difference between the calculations for parametric tests and for non-parametric tests is that, instead of adding up *ranks*, all the *scores* in ANOVA have to be squared. For the more complex ANOVA designs described in Chapter 15, we will be recommending computerized statistical packages. These are now widely available and can be used by anyone who has access to a computer. Guidance will be given in later chapters. However, those of you who are studying this book on your own certainly do not need to despair. These statistical tests were invented many years ago before the advent of modern computers so you will be no worse off than the many thousands of students who have carried out statistical calculations using an ordinary calculator. In any case, it is important to carry out the calculations for at least one ANOVA 'by hand' – with the help of a calculator, of course. This will help you to gain a real understanding of the underlying principles involved in working out *F* ratios.

13.2 One-way ANOVA (unrelated)

When to use

This analysis is used when a *single variable* is tested under *three or more* conditions and different subjects are used for each of the conditions (an

Table 13.2   Number of words recalled (unrelated)

	Condition 1 (slow rate)	Condition 2 (medium rate)	Condition 3 (fast rate)	
	8	7	4	
	7	8	5	
	9	5	3	
	5	4	6	
	6	6	2	
	8	7	4	
Totals (T)	43	37	24	104 Grand total
Means	7.17	6.17	4	

unrelated design). As you can see from Decision Chart 2, the one-way unrelated ANOVA is the parametric equivalent of the non-parametric Kruskal–Wallis test for *unrelated designs* with *three or more conditions.*

Sample data

Three different groups of six subjects were given lists of ten words to learn, the first group at a slow rate of presentation of one word every 5 seconds, the second group at a medium rate of 2 seconds per word and the third group at a fast rate of one word every second. The recall scores are shown in Table 13.2.

Hypothesis

The experimenters predicted that the three conditions of presentation rate would have an effect on recall scores.

ANOVA sources of variance table

Table 13.3 shows the appropriate form of ANOVA table for this experiment. There is one independent variable between conditions (presentation rate) and three experimental conditions (slow, medium, fast) as shown in Table 13.3. The differences between the three conditions contribute to the variance for SS_{bet}.

Table 13.3 One-way ANOVA (unrelated)

Sources of variance	Sums of squares	Degrees of freedom	Mean squares	F ratio
Presentation rate (between conditions)	SS_{bet}	df_{bet}	$\dfrac{SS_{bet}}{df_{bet}}$	$\dfrac{MS_{bet}}{MS_{error}}$
Error	SS_{error}	df_{error}	$\dfrac{SS_{error}}{df_{error}}$	
Total	SS_{tot}	df_{tot}		

Rationale

The presentation rate independent variable represents the predicted differences in recall scores *between* the three conditions. Any differences between subjects due to other irrelevant variables is represented by the *error variance*. The *F* ratio represents a test of the experimental hypothesis that the variance *between* conditions will be relatively large compared with the error variance due to irrelevant variables.

Preparing the data

For one-way (unrelated) ANOVA the scores for the three (or more) conditions are set out as shown in Table 13.2. Remember that it is essential to calculate the means, although they will not be needed for ANOVA calculations. So often students calculate the variances in the scores and look up the significance of the *F* ratio. But, because they have not calculated the means, they forget the direction of any difference. The means in Table 13.2 show that the slow rate of presentation produced the highest recall, the medium rate the next highest and the fast rate the least. The aim of ANOVA is to decide whether these differences are significant.

If you find any of the symbols used in the step-by-step instructions problematical look back to Chapter 11, Section 11.3.

Step-by-step instructions for calculating one-way *F* (unrelated)

These are given in Box K.

Box K

Step-by-step instructions for calculating one-way F ratios (unrelated)

1   Note the following symbols
     (see Table 13.2):

  $\sum T^2$ = sum of squared totals $43^2 + 37^2 + 24^2$
          for each condition

   n = number of subjects in $n = 6$
           each condition

   N = total number of scores $N = 18$

  $(\sum x)^2$ = grand total squared $(\sum x)^2 = 104^2$

  $\dfrac{(\sum x)^2}{N}$ = constant to be $\dfrac{104^2}{18} = \dfrac{10816}{18} = 600.89$
          subtracted from all
          sums of squares

  $\sum x^2$ = sum of each individual
          score squared

2   Calculate SS_{bet}

  $\dfrac{\sum T^2}{n} - \dfrac{(\sum x)^2}{N}$ $= \dfrac{43^2 + 37^2 + 24^2}{6} - 600.89$

            $= 632.33 - 600.89$

            $= 31.44$

3   Calculate SS_{tot}

  $\sum x^2 - \dfrac{(\sum x)^2}{N}$ $= 8^2 + 7^2 + 9^2 + 5^2 + 6^2$

            $+\ 8^2 + 7^2 + 8^2 + 5^2 + 4^2$

            $+\ 6^2 + 7^2 + 4^2 + 5^2 + 3^2$

            $+\ 6^2 + 2^2 + 4^2 - 600.89$

            $= 664 - 600.89$

            $= 63.11$

4   Calculate SS_{error}

  $SS_{\text{tot}} - SS_{\text{bet}}$ $= 63.11 - 31.44$

            $= 31.67$

5   Calculate the degrees of freedom

  df_{bet} = number of conditions $- 1$ $df_{\text{bet}} = 3 - 1 = 2$

  $df_{\text{tot}} = N - 1$ $df_{\text{tot}} = 18 - 1 = 17$

  $df_{\text{error}} = df_{\text{tot}} - df_{\text{bet}}$ $df_{\text{error}} = 17 - 2 = 15$

6   Divide each *SS* by *df* to obtain *MS*

$$MS_{bet} = \frac{SS_{bet}}{df_{bet}} \qquad = \frac{31.44}{2} = 15.72$$

$$MS_{error} = \frac{SS_{error}}{df_{error}} \qquad = \frac{31.67}{15} = 2.11$$

7   Calculate the *F* ratio for MS_{bet} over MS_{error} allocating the correct *df* to MS_{bet} and MS_{error}

$$F \text{ ratio for } MS_{bet} = \frac{MS_{bet}}{MS_{error}} \qquad F_{2,15} = \frac{15.72}{2.11} = 7.45$$

8   The completed ANOVA table is shown in Table 13.4.

Table 13.4   One-way ANOVA table (unrelated)

Sources of variance	Sums of squares	Degrees of freedom	Mean squares	F ratio
Presentation rate	31.44	2	15.72	$F_{2,15} = 7.45$
Error	31.67	15	2.11	
Total	63.11	17		

Looking up the significance of *F* in Table J

To be significant the calculated value of the statistic *F* has to be *equal to* or *larger than* the values in Tables J. To look up the significance of the observed value of *F* we use Tables J(1)–J(4). Each of the tables gives the critical value of *F* for a different level of significance. Table J(1) shows the values of *F* at the $p < 0.05$ level; Table J(2) at the $p < 0.025$ level; Table J(3) at the $p < 0.01$ level; and Table J(4) at the $p < 0.001$ level.

We need to know the *degrees of freedom* to locate the values of *F* in the tables. The two degrees of freedom that we use are df_{bet} and df_{error} (2 and 15, respectively). That is why the *F* ratio is shown as $F_{2,15}$ in the ANOVA table. In Table J(1) df_{bet} is shown along the v_1 row and df_{error} is shown down the v_2 column. Locate 2 on the v_1 row and follow the v_2 column down until you find 15. In Table J(1) the value of $F_{2,15}$ is 3.68 for $p < 0.05$ level of significance. Since the calculated *F* value of 7.45 is larger than 3.68, we can reject the null hypothesis and conclude that rate of presentation has a significant effect on recall of words. Note that *df* for the variable is always v_1 and *df* for the error is always v_2.

The next step is to see whether the calculated value of *F* is significant at the levels of significance given in Tables J(2)–J(4). Our calculated *F* of 7.45 is significant at the $p < 0.025$ and $p < 0.01$ levels of significance because it is larger than the values of $F_{2,15}$ in Tables J(2) and J(3), 4.76 and 6.36, respectively. However, it is not significant at the $p < 0.001$ level of significance because the calculated value of 7.45 is smaller than the value for $F_{2,15}$ of 11.34 in Table J(4).

Conclusions

There are significant differences between the three experimental conditions ($p < 0.01$). This supports the experimental hypothesis that presentation rate affects recall scores for words. You should notice that ANOVA only decides whether there are overall significant differences between the experimental conditions. In a sense ANOVA only tests two-tailed hypotheses that there are significant differences between conditions.

Question 42 (a) Analyse the data in Table 13.5 for a one-way unrelated design. Follow the step-by-step instructions in Box K for calculating *F* and producing an ANOVA table.

(b) Look up *F* using the appropriate *df* in Table J.

(c) What other parametric test could have been used to analyse the data in Table 13.5?

Table 13.5   Data for one-way unrelated ANOVA

	Variable A		
	A_1	A_2	
	4	3	
	8	2	
	7	1	
	6	4	
	5	7	
Totals	30	17	47 Grand total

One-way ANOVA (related)

When to use

This analysis is used when a *single variable* is tested under *three or more conditions* and the same subjects are used for all experimental conditions (a *related design*). As indicated in Decision Chart 2, the one-way related ANOVA is the parametric equivalent of the non-parametric Friedman test for *related designs* with *three or more conditions.*

Sample data

We are going to use the same experimental results as in Section 13.2. But this time we assume that the *same* six subjects are doing all three experimental conditions, learning different lists of words under slow, medium and fast rates of presentation. The results are shown in Table 13.6. The number for each subject in the left-hand column indicates that this time there are three scores for each subject.

Hypothesis

The experimenter predicted that the independent variable of presentation rate would result in differences between conditions.

Table 13.6 Number of words recalled (related design)

Subjects	Condition 1 (slow rate)	Condition 2 (medium rate)	Condition 3 (fast rate)	Totals for subjects (T_s)
1	8	7	4	19
2	7	8	5	20
3	9	5	3	17
4	5	4	6	15
5	6	6	2	14
6	8	7	4	19
Totals (T)	43	37	24	104 Grand total
Means	7.17	6.17	4	

Table 13.7   One-way ANOVA (related)

Sources of variance	Sums of squares	Degrees of freedom	Mean squares	F ratios
Presentation rate (between conditions)	SS_{bet}	df_{bet}	$\dfrac{SS_{bet}}{df_{bet}}$	$\dfrac{MS_{bet}}{MS_{error}}$
Subjects	SS_{subj}	df_{subj}	$\dfrac{SS_{subj}}{df_{subj}}$	$\dfrac{MS_{subj}}{MS_{error}}$
Error	SS_{error}	df_{error}	$\dfrac{SS_{error}}{df_{error}}$	
Total	SS_{tot}	df_{tot}		

ANOVA sources of variance table

The big difference between related ANOVA and unrelated ANOVA is that in a related design all subjects are doing all conditions. As in all related designs, a comparison can be made between subjects' performance under the three conditions. In ANOVA this means that there are *four* sources of variance. The extra source of variance is due to variability between subjects.

In Table 13.7 there are *four* sources of variance. The first is SS_{bet}, which represents the predicted differences between the three presentation rate conditions. The second source of variance is SS_{subj}, which represents the differences between subjects over all three conditions. SS_{error} represents unpredictable error variance even after the variance between subjects has been accounted for. SS_{tot} is the total variance which is the sum of all sources of variance.

Rationale

The general method for calculating the sums of squares for each source of variance is exactly the same as that used for the unrelated ANOVA design, except that we have to calculate an additional sum of squares for subjects. We shall again be calculating each sum of squares by summing together squared scores and subtracting the same *constant*, the grand total of scores squared divided by the total number of scores in the table. The *F* ratio represents the size of the variance due to the experimental conditions in relation to error variance.

Preparing the data

For one-way related ANOVA the scores should be set out as in Table 13.6. Remember to calculate the means. In Table 13.6 the totals for each condition (T) have been added up; these will be used for calculating the differences between conditions (SS_{bet}). This time the totals for each subject (T_s) have also been added up across each horizontal row; these will be used to calculate the differences between subjects (SS_{subj}). The grand total has also been calculated to be divided by N for the constant. As we are using the same data as for the unrelated ANOVA in Section 13.2 it is not surprising that the constant is the same for both sets of data.

Step-by-step instructions for calculating F (related)

These are given in Box L (overleaf).

Looking up the significance of F in Table J

The F ratios indicate the appropriate degrees of freedom for consulting Table J. Starting with Table J(1), we locate the degrees of freedom for between conditions (df_{bet}) along the v_1 row and the degrees of freedom for the error (df_{error}) down the v_2 column. Where they intersect is the value of F for these df. In our example, $v_1 = 2$, $v_2 = 10$ (see page 131), and the F value is 4.10. Since our calculated F of 7.18 is *larger* than this, we can reject the null hypothesis and conclude that there is a significant effect of presentation rate on recall ($p < 0.05$). If you look at Tables J(2)–J(4), you will see that our calculated $F_{2,10}$ of 7.18 is larger than the value of 5.46 in Table J(2) but not the value of 7.56 in Table J(3). So the predicted effects of presentation rate are significant at $p < 0.025$ but not at $p < 0.01$.

You will notice that in the step-by-step instructions the F ratio for subjects was also calculated. The degrees of freedom are $6 - 1 = 5$ (because there were six subjects doing all three conditions) and 10 for the error variance. Despite the fact that it is possible to separate out the differences due to each subject's performance in related ANOVA designs this still counts as undesirable variance. Researchers hope that they have eliminated variance due to subjects by counterbalancing the order in which subjects did the conditions. For this reason, it is common practice to test the significance of the F ratio for subjects, hoping that it will *not* be a significant source of variance. In our example the calculated $F_{5,10}$ of 0.8935 is much smaller than the value of 3.33 in Table J(1) and so the differences between subjects are not significant.

Box L

Step-by-step instructions for calculating one-way F ratios (related)

1   Note the following symbols
     (see Table 13.6):

$\sum T^2$ = sum of squared total for each condition $\sum T^2 = 43^2 + 37^2 + 24^2$

$\sum T_s^2$ = sum of squared totals for each subject $\sum T_s^2 = 19^2 + 20^2 + 17^2 + 15^2 + 14^2 + 19^2$

n = number of subjects $n = 6$

c = number of conditions $c = 3$

N = total number of scores $N = 18$

$(\sum x)^2$ = grand total squared $(\sum x)^2 = 104^2$

$\dfrac{(\sum x)^2}{N}$ = constant to be subtracted from all SS $\dfrac{104^2}{18} = \dfrac{10816}{18} = 600.89$

$\sum x^2$ = sum of each individual score squared

2   Calculate SS_{bet}

$$\frac{\sum T^2}{n} - \frac{(\sum x)^2}{N}$$

$$= \frac{43^2 + 37^2 + 24^2}{6} - 600.89$$

$$= 632.33 - 600.89$$

$$= 31.44$$

3   Calculate SS_{subj}

$$\frac{\sum T_s^2}{c} - \frac{(\sum x)^2}{N}$$

$$= \frac{19^2 + 20^2 + 17^2 + 15^2 + 14^2 + 19^2}{3}$$

$$- 600.89$$

$$= 610.67 - 600.89$$

$$= 9.78$$

4   Calculate SS_{tot}

$$\sum x^2 - \frac{(\sum x)^2}{N}$$

$$= 8^2 + 7^2 + 9^2 + 5^2 + 6^2 + 8^2 + 7^2$$
$$+ 8^2 + 5^2 + 4^2 + 6^2 + 7^2 + 4^2 + 5^2$$
$$+ 3^2 + 6^2 + 2^2 + 4^2 - 600.89$$

$$= 664 - 600.89$$

$$= 63.11$$

5   Calculate SS_{error}

$SS_{tot} - SS_{bet} - SS_{subj}$ $= 63.11 - 31.44 - 9.78$

                                     $= 21.89$

6   Calculate the degrees of freedom

df_{bet} = number of conditions − 1 $df_{bet} = 3 - 1 = 2$

df_{subj} = number of subjects − 1 $df_{subj} = 6 - 1 = 5$

$df_{tot} = N - 1$ $df_{tot} = 18 - 1 = 17$

$df_{error} = df_{tot} - df_{bet} - df_{subj}$ $df_{error} = 17 - 2 - 5 = 10$

7   Divide each *SS* by *df* to obtain *MS*

$$MS_{bet} = \frac{SS_{bet}}{df_{bet}} \qquad\qquad = \frac{31.44}{2} = 15.72$$

$$MS_{subj} = \frac{SS_{subj}}{df_{subj}} \qquad\qquad = \frac{9.78}{5} = 1.956$$

$$MS_{error} = \frac{SS_{error}}{df_{error}} \qquad\qquad = \frac{21.89}{10} = 2.189$$

8   Calculate *F* ratios for MS_{bet} over MS_{error} and for MS_{subj} over MS_{error} allocating the correct *df* to the *F* ratios:

$$F \text{ ratio for } MS_{bet} = \frac{MS_{bet}}{MS_{error}} \qquad F_{2,10} = \frac{15.72}{2.189} = 7.18$$

$$F \text{ ratio for } MS_{subj} = \frac{MS_{subj}}{MS_{error}} \qquad F_{5,10} = \frac{1.956}{2.189} = 0.8935$$

9   The completed ANOVA is shown in Table 13.8.

Table 13.8   One-way ANOVA table (related)

Sources of variance	Sums of squares	Degrees of freedom	Mean squares	F ratios
Presentation rate	31.44	2	15.72	$F_{2,10} = 7.18$
Subjects	9.78	5	1.956	$F_{5,10} = 0.8935$
Error	21.89	10	2.189	
Total	63.11	17		

Conclusions

The results show overall significant differences due to presentation rates ($p < 0.025$).

? **Question 43** (a) Analyse the data in Table 13.9 following the step-by-step instructions in Box L for a one-way related design.

(b) Are the results significant? If so, at what level of significance?

Table 13.9   Data for one-way related ANOVA

| Subjects | Variable A | | Total |
	A_1	A_2	
1	3	2	5
2	6	4	10
3	4	3	7
4	9	3	12
5	5	4	9
Totals	27	16	43

14 Multivariable experimental designs

14.1 Single-variable designs

In Chapters 1 and 2 you were introduced to the basic principles of research and experimental design. Experiments are designed to investigate the effects of independent variables on dependent variables. The experimental hypothesis predicts the effect of an independent variable on the dependent variable (subjects' scores) as opposed to the null hypothesis that there will be only random differences in scores. One important source of random variability is caused by individual differences in people's performance. This has to be taken into account when deciding whether to use the same subjects in all conditions or different subjects in each condition.

If anything in this recap of the issues relevant to experimental designs seems puzzling, reread Chapters 1 and 2 to refresh your memory about the importance of controlling variability.

The most important feature of the experimental designs discussed in Chapter 2 is that they are only able to consider *one* independent variable. There might be several conditions but these are relevant to the manipulation of a single variable. For instance, it was only possible to investigate the effects of reading schemes or the effects of whether words are rare or common. This is why such experiments are called **single-variable designs**.

The same applies to the parametric tests we have covered so far. The *t* tests in Chapter 12 were concerned with differences between two conditions due to a single variable. The one-way ANOVA designs in Chapter 13 could only test a single variable for three or more conditions. Another way of putting it is that for all these designs there was only one between-conditions variable. This is why in Decision Chart 2 inside the *back cover* the *t* tests and one-way ANOVA are both found on the *left-hand branch* where a one-variable design has been selected.

14.2 Multivariable designs

You will remember that right back in the Prologue the 'sceptical teacher' expresses an interest in whether the reading scheme was more effective for less good readers or good readers. The problem is that in order to test this it would be necessary to look at *two* independent variables at once: (a) whether children are good or less good readers; *and* (b) the effect of the reading scheme.

In single-variable designs it is only possible to investigate one independent variable at a time, for example, the reading scheme variable. If there was a possibility that good and less good readers might affect the result, all that could be done is to ensure that good and poor readers are distributed equally as subjects in the two conditions so that they would not bias the results.

In multivariable designs it is possible to investigate *two or more independent variables* at once. This is why they are called **multivariable designs**. In this type of design it is possible to investigate the effects of the reading scheme, the performance of good and less good readers and the crucial question of whether good and less good readers are affected by the reading scheme in different ways. This possibility that there might be a differential effect of one independent variable on another is one of the great advantages of multivariable designs. These differential effects are known as *interactions* between the two variables. Interactions will be fully discussed in the justification for multivariable experimental designs.

Table 14.1 shows the effects of two independent variables, each of which has two conditions. The first independent variable is our old friend the reading scheme (variable *A*: reading scheme or no reading scheme). The second independent variable is reading skills (variable *B*: good or less good readers). The combinations of the two variables result in *four conditions* as shown in Table 14.1. Condition 1 shows the combination of less good readers with no reading scheme; condition 2, good readers with no reading scheme; condition 3, less good readers with a reading scheme; and condition 4, good readers with a reading scheme. This makes it possible to compare whether good readers benefit from a reading scheme (condition 2 versus condition 4) or whether less good readers benefit from the reading scheme (condition 1 versus condition 3).

Table 14.1 Four conditions in a multivariable design

Condition 1	Condition 2	Condition 3	Condition 4
Less good readers	Good readers	Less good readers	Good readers
No reading scheme	No reading scheme	Reading scheme	Reading scheme

Table 14.2   2 × 2 table for four conditions

Variable B: *Reading skills*	*Variable A: Reading schemes*	
	No reading scheme	*Reading scheme*
Less good readers	Condition 1	Condition 3
Good readers	Condition 2	Condition 4

14.3   Two-by-two tables

In order to demonstrate that a multivariable design is varying two independent variables, they are usually expressed as **two-by-two tables**. These are also called *2 × 2 tables*. In these tables each of the independent variables is shown separately so that the effects of the two variables can be identified. The **2 × 2 table** in Table 14.2 is another way of displaying the experimental conditions given in Table 14.1.

The top left-hand box represents condition 1 in Table 14.1: less good readers (variable *B*) who are not given a reading scheme (variable *A*). The top right-hand box represents condition 3: less good readers with a reading scheme.

? Question 44   'Boxes' in 2 × 2 tables are usually labelled as *cells* so that there is no need to refer to the 'top left-hand box'. Suppose the boxes in Table 14.2 are labelled as cells 1 to 4, as shown in Table 14.3. Which are the appropriate cells in Table 14.3 for the four conditions in Table 14.1?

Table 14.3   Labelled cells in 2 × 2 table

	No reading scheme	*Reading scheme*
Less good readers	Cell 1	Cell 3
Good readers	Cell 2	Cell 4

Table 14.4 2×2 table of scores

Variable B   *Variable A*

	No reading scheme	*Reading scheme*	Totals
Less good readers	2	7	9
Good readers	8	8	16
Totals	10	15	

The next step is to put some numbers into the 2×2 table. Let us suppose that we had carried out an experiment and had calculated the scores for each of the four conditions in Table 14.1. These scores have been entered into the appropriate cells in Table 14.4. The totals for the variable A conditions and for the variable B conditions have also been calculated.

The total for both conditions in which there is no reading scheme adds up the scores for both the less good readers (2) and the good readers (8): $2 + 8 = 10$. The equivalent total for conditions in which there is a reading scheme is the total of less good readers (7) and good readers (8), adding up to 15.

The differences between the totals for no reading scheme (10) and reading scheme (15) shows the overall difference between these two conditions regardless of whether the children were good or less good readers. This overall difference is known as a **main effect** because it compares the overall scores for variable A (no reading scheme versus reading scheme).

? Question 45 Which main effect is represented by the totals of 9 and 16 at the right-hand side of Table 14.4?

14.4   Interpreting interactions

It is obviously interesting to look at the main effects in a 2×2 experiment as shown in Table 14.4. These represent the differences between the effects of variable A, no reading scheme versus reading scheme (total scores of 10 versus 15 showing the main effect of higher scores for the reading scheme). Table 14.4 also shows the differences between variable *B*, less good and good readers (9 versus 16 showing the main effect of good readers performing better). However, it could be argued that these main effects could just as well have been demonstrated in two single experiments. One experiment could have looked at performance with and without the reading scheme. Another separate experiment could have looked at the performance of less good and good readers.

In contrast, the whole point of a **multivariable experiment** is that *two independent variables* can be investigated *simultaneously* to see whether the two variables influence each other. Do less good readers benefit more from a reading scheme than good readers? What we want to know is whether it is the less good or the good readers who benefited most from the reading scheme.

Let us suppose that the experimental hypothesis was that less good readers would benefit more whereas the good readers were already so good at reading that they would not benefit so much from a reading scheme. If you look at Table 14.4 it is clear that the performance of the good readers is better than the less good readers overall (scores of 16 versus 9). But, if you look at the individual cells in the table you will see that the scores for the good readers are no different regardless of whether they had a reading scheme or not (8 versus 8). On the other hand, the less good readers, when given a reading scheme, improved from a total of 2 up to a total of 7.

This could be interpreted as showing that good readers are unlikely to show an improvement due to a reading scheme while less good readers are likely to improve their reading performance when they are given a reading scheme. Another way of expressing this is that performance on variable *A* (no reading scheme versus reading scheme) is *influenced* by the effects of variable *B* (good or less good readers). It is only the less good readers whose performance is affected by the reading scheme. The fact that performance on one variable is affected by performance on the other variable demonstrates that there is an **interaction** between the two variables. Interactions are often thought to be a very difficult concept to grasp. But all they mean is that two independent variables interact in the sense that one independent variable is influenced by another variable. An alternative way of putting this is that subjects behave differently on one of the variables as a direct result of the second variable.

14.5   Using graphs to investigate interactions

One good way of indicating whether there is an interaction between variables is to draw **graphs** of the data (as in Figure 14.1). How should one set about drawing a graph? Every graph has a vertical line and a horizontal line. Each line of the graph is called an *axis* (plural *axes*). The vertical axis

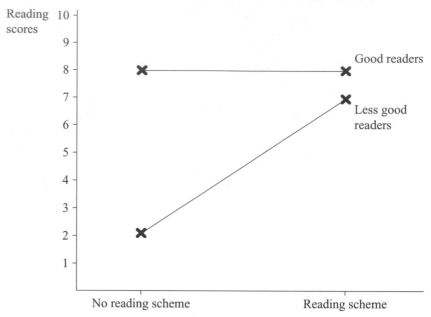

Figure 14.1   Graph showing interaction

is labelled 'Reading scores' and the horizontal axis 'No reading scheme' and 'Reading scheme'.

The aim is to plot the reading scores of the less good and good readers against the no reading scheme and reading scheme conditions. We use the scores in Table 14.4. For good readers the reading scores were 8 for both the no reading scheme and reading scheme conditions. As a result, scores for good readers are both plotted against the score of 8 on the reading scores axis. For less good readers the reading scores were 2 for no reading scheme and 7 for the reading scheme so for less good readers their reading scores are plotted at 2 and 7 on the left-hand vertical axis.

In order to demonstrate whether there is an interaction the normal practice is to draw lines connecting the reading scores for good and less good readers. The line connecting the reading scores for the good readers is flat because these readers got exactly the same score whether they were given a reading scheme or not. In contrast, the line connecting the scores for less good readers shows a definite slope, rising from 2 for the no reading scheme condition to 7 for the reading scheme condition. The rising line demonstrates an improvement in reading scores for the less good readers. The question is whether the difference in the *slopes* of the lines is sufficiently large to decide that there is an *interaction* between the scores of the two groups.

To show an example when there is no interaction, let us suppose the scores for the four conditions shown in Table 14.5 are plotted on the graph in Figure 14.2. In this case, the lines connecting the plotted scores of 2

Table 14.5   2 × 2 tables of scores

	No reading scheme	*Reading scheme*	Totals
Less good readers	2	7	9
Good readers	4	9	13
Totals	6	16	

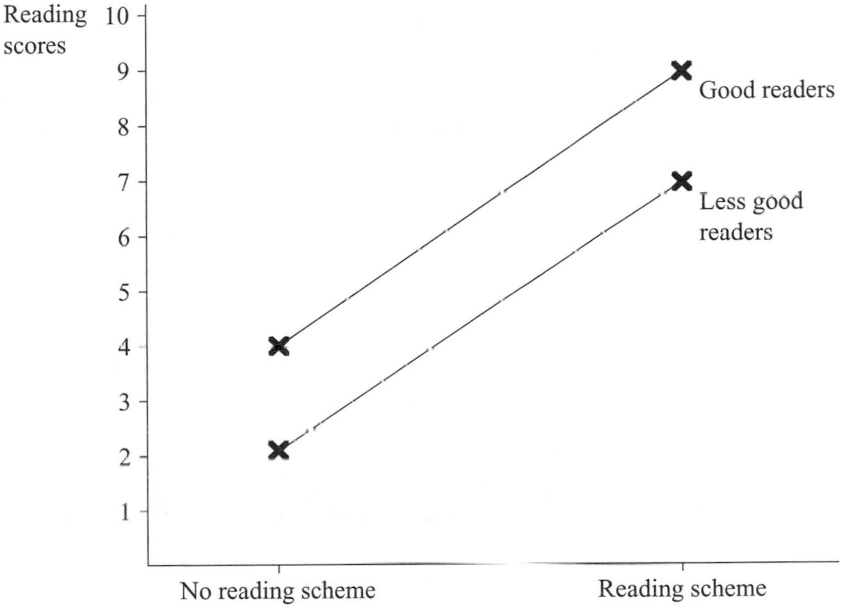

Figure 14.2   Graph showing no interaction

and 7 for less good readers and 4 and 9 for good readers have exactly the same slope. Good readers have higher reading scores than less good readers and having a reading scheme leads to higher scores than not having a reading scheme. These are both main effects of variables *A* and *B* and are not particularly surprising. But here there is no hint of any interaction between the two variables. Both groups of readers have shown the same amount of improvement from the reading scheme.

You will probably have realized that a graph is simply another way of representing a 2 × 2 table. The graph in Figure 14.1 is equivalent to the 2 × 2 table of scores in Table 14.4, and the graph in Figure 14.2 is equivalent to Table 14.5.

Sometimes an interaction can be even more dramatic when performance on one variable goes in the opposite direction depending on the effects of

Table 14.6   Four conditions of texts and titles

Condition 1	Condition 2	Condition 3	Condition 4
Title 'furniture'	Title 'furniture'	Title 'animals'	Title 'animals'
Text animals	Text furniture	Text animals	Text furniture

another variable. Suppose the experimental hypothesis was that people who are given a title which is compatible with the content of a text would be more likely to remember it than people who are given an incompatible title. Subjects were given a text which was either about furniture or animals. One group were given a text about animals with a compatible title 'animals', the other group was given the animal text with the incompatible title 'furniture'. Corresponding groups were given a text about furniture with either a compatible title 'furniture' or an incompatible title 'animals'. The design is shown in Table 14.6.

? Question 46 (a) According to the experimental hypothesis, which of the conditions listed in Table 14.6 would be expected to result in more text being remembered?

(b) The means for the four conditions in Table 14.6 have been arranged as a 2 × 2 table in Table 14.7.

Looking at the recall scores in Table 14.7, are there likely to be:

(i) Differences in recall between furniture and animals texts?

(ii) Differences between 'furniture' and 'animals' titles?

(iii) Is there any reason to expect either of these main effects?

Table 14.7   2 × 2 table of recall scores for texts and titles

	Variable A (title)		
Variable B (text)	Title 'furniture'	Title 'animals'	Totals
Text furniture	20	5	25
Text animals	5	20	25
Totals	25	25	

(c) Draw a graph showing recall scores on the vertical axis and furniture and animals titles on the horizontal axis. Plot the total recall scores for the two texts and draw lines between them.

The crux of this experiment is to show an *interaction* between variable *A* (title) and variable *B* (text). The hypothesis is that there will be an interaction depending on whether the text and title are compatible or incompatible. This is an example in which the hypothesis predicts an interaction and is not concerned with main effects. Any main effect differences, for instance, animal texts in general being easier to remember than furniture texts, would need to be explained.

The purpose of the two-way ANOVA designs which will be described in Chapter 15 is to analyse the experimental data from multivariable experiments to test the significance of main effects and interactions.

 Progress box twelve

Multivariable designs

- In single-variable designs only *one independent variable* can be varied at a time.
- In multivariable designs *two or more independent variables* can be investigated simultaneously.
- This makes it possible to study the *main effects* for each independent variable.
- It is also possible to discover whether there is an *interaction* showing that behaviour on one independent variable is influenced by another independent variable.
- *Graphs* are a good method for demonstrating the presence or absence of an interaction.
- *Two-way ANOVA* can test the significance of main effects and interactions.

14.6   Using Decision Chart 2

In Decision Chart 2 inside the *back cover* of the book, if you follow the diamond box down from 'Differences between conditions?' the next diamond asks 'One variable or two or more variables?' So far we have only been directed to the left-hand branch for single-variable designs, like the *t* test and one-way ANOVA. But with the introduction of multivariable designs it is now possible to opt for two or more variables. The left-hand branch for single-variable designs demonstrates that the *t* test and one-way ANOVA are parametric alternatives to the simpler rank-based non-parametric tests. The *right-hand branch* for two or more variables can only be handled by parametric ANOVA tests which can deal with more than one variable at a time.

Two-way ANOVA allows researchers to test more sophisticated experimental hypotheses. They may predict that a reading scheme will help everyone to some extent. They may predict that good readers will in general be better than less good readers. But in a two-way design they can also predict that one independent variable will influence another independent variable. Good readers may be better at reading but less good readers who have been given a reading scheme may show more improvement. The prediction that there will be an *interaction* between two independent variables is only possible in a multivariable design which can test both variables simultaneously.

14.7   Computerized statistical packages

It is possible to carry out all the calculations for two-way ANOVA using a calculator which automatically squares numbers and adds up the sum of squares. The principles of calculating sums of squares by subtracting a constant; dividing by *df* to calculate mean squares; comparing predicted mean squares against error variance to calculate *F* ratios; looking up *F* ratios in Table J – all these are identical to the calculations used for one-way ANOVA. The only problem is that these calculations have to be carried out for more sources of variance.

Because of the extra numerical work, computer packages have been devised to do these calculations for you. This may seem too good to be true. But there are a few health warnings, and by this I am not referring to the dangers of sitting in front of a computer screen. The first of these is that researchers often type scores into a computer statistical package and out comes a set of *F* ratios with their probabilities. The danger is that the experimenter forgets the experimental hypothesis which was the purpose of setting up the experiment and, even worse, the direction in which the means were supposed to differ.

First word of advice: be very clear about your experimental hypothesis and the predicted differences.

Second word of advice: draw up a table of scores for all conditions and calculate the means to see whether they are in the right direction to support your hypothesis.

The crucial issue for all statistical computer packages is to understand what data you should type in. The program needs to know whether you have used the same subjects or different subjects for the experimental conditions. This is to enable it to treat the analysis as related or unrelated. The program will also need to know how many conditions and how many subjects you have used for each condition.

Our intention is not to give you acres and acres of program codes for using each of these packages. They all have slightly different formats and a lot depends on the kind of machine you have available, whether this is one of your own or one that is available at your university or place of work. Because the terminology used is sometimes slightly different, we have supplied a glossary of equivalent terms used by the most commonly used statistical package in Appendix 1.

Third word of advice: draw up a 2 × 2 table so that you understand the structure of the data you will be inputting to the statistical package.

Once you have input the scores in the correct order, the program will work out for each source of variance the appropriate sums of squares, calculate the *df*s from the numbers of conditions and subjects and make all the necessary calculations to obtain an *F* ratio for each source of variance. Most programs will also work out the levels of significance for each *F* ratio and generate a graph of results.

Fourth word of advice: draw up a labelled graph of your own scores to help you understand your data (even if the computer does one for you).

It is only if you have understood the rationale of the experiment, the structure of the experimental conditions and the appropriate data for each condition that you will be able to understand the output of a computer program. You have to know what sources of variance have been used to produce *F* ratios in order to decide whether the differences predicted by the experimental hypothesis have been supported.

Fifth word of advice: check any significance levels against your original means and 2 × 2 table.

15 Two-way ANOVA

15.1 Two-way ANOVA tables

Because two variables are being investigated in the same experiment, a two-way ANOVA must be able to identify the sources of variance for both variables. It is inevitable that two-way ANOVA tables are more complex because there are more predicted sources of variance, one for each variable and one for the predicted interaction between the two variables. Table 15.1 shows each source of variance and its associated F ratio. This table expresses the fact that all sources of variance must add up to the total variance in subjects' scores. It also shows that F ratios can be calculated for each source of variance separately.

In effect, the between-subjects variance in a one-way ANOVA has been divided up into *three* sources of variance: variable A variance, variable B variance and $A \times B$ interaction variance. As with one-way ANOVA, the basic method is to sum squares of individual and total scores, and divide by the appropriate degrees of freedom to calculate mean squares and F ratios.

Degrees of freedom

The degrees of freedom are more complicated to calculate when there are more sources of variance. But the general rule is the same, that degrees of freedom are based on $C - 1$, $N - 1$ and $n - 1$, because the last score in a condition or a group of subjects is predictable and therefore cannot vary.

Reread Chapter 11, Section 11.5, to refresh your memory about the general principles underlying degrees of freedom.

The problem comes when calculating degrees of freedom for interactions. In this case, there are degrees of freedom for each independent variable, both of which are relevant to the interaction between the variables. The rule is that the *df* for each independent variable is multiplied to arrive at the *df* for the interaction.

Table 15.1 ANOVA table for two variables

Sources of variance	F ratios
Variable A	$\dfrac{\text{variance due to variable } A}{\text{error variance}}$
Variable B	$\dfrac{\text{variance due to variable } B}{\text{error variance}}$
Interaction $A \times B$	$\dfrac{\text{variance due to interaction } A \times B}{\text{error variance}}$
Error variance	
Total variance	

The rules for calculating *df* are shown in Table 15.2. Check that the individual degrees of freedom add up to the total *df*.

Table 15.2 ANOVA table for two variables: degrees of freedom

Source of variance	Degrees of freedom (df)
Variable A (2 conditions)	$2 - 1 = 1$
Variable B (2 conditions)	$2 - 1 = 1$
Interaction $A \times B$	$1 \times 1 = 1$
Error	$19 - 1 - 1 - 1 = 16$
Total (20 subjects)	$20 - 1 = 19$

Preparing data for two-way ANOVA

The first step is to set up a table showing the scores for the subjects and the means for each condition. For two-way ANOVA designs the conditions have to be arranged to represent each of the variables in the form of a hierarchy (see Table 15.3). In this case the two variables are variable A (two types of textbooks, X and Y) and variable B (short or long study periods).

For ANOVA these scores need to be arranged as a 2×2 table, as shown in Table 15.4. The two variables are now shown one along the top of the table and one down the left-hand side. The four cells of the table represent the four conditions and the scores are arranged accordingly.

Table 15.3   Tables of scores for two variables

	Textbook X		Textbook Y	
	Short period (condition 1)	*Long period (condition 2)*	*Short period (condition 3)*	*Long period (condition 4)*
	2	4	7	10
	3	5	8	11
	4	6	9	12
Means				

Table 15.4   2 × 2 table of scores

	Variable A	
	Textbook X	*Textbook Y*
Variable B	Cell 1	Cell 2
Short study period	2	7
	3	8
	4	9
	Cell 3	Cell 4
	4	10
Long study period	5	11
	6	12

? Question 47   (a)   Calculate the means in Table 15.3.

(b)   Check that the conditions in Table 15.3 have been transferred to the correct cells in Table 15.4.

15.2   Two-way ANOVA (unrelated)

When to use

This analysis is used when *two variables* are tested with *two or more* conditions for each variable and *different* subjects are used for each of the conditions.

Table 15.5 Recall scores for two variables (unrelated)

Variable B (rate of presentation)	Variable A (word length)		Totals B
	A_1 (short words)	A_2 (long words)	
B_1 *(fast rate)*	9 8 6 7	5 3 3 4	
	30	15	45
B_2 *(slow rate)*	4 3 3 5	7 5 6 7	
	15	25	40
Totals A	45	40	Grand total 85

Sample data

Sixteen different subjects are allocated four each to four experimental conditions. The four conditions represent two conditions for each of two variables: word length and rate of presentation. Four subjects are given a list of short words presented at a fast rate; four subjects are given a list of short words presented at a slow rate; four subjects are given a list of long words presented at a fast rate; and four subjects are given a list of long words presented as a slow rate. The recall scores are presented in a 2×2 table in Table 15.5.

Notice that there are *equal* numbers of subjects in each condition, a necessary assumption for all the formulae given below. We have added up the totals for each of the four conditions (30, 15, 15, 25), the totals for the two conditions for variable A (45, 40) and for variable B (which also happen to be 45, 40) and the grand total (85).

 Question 48 Check that all the scores, the four cell totals, the bottom and side totals all add up to the grand total of 85.

Hypothesis

It was predicted that there would be a significant interaction between the two variables, with more short words being recalled at a fast rate of

Table 15.6   Two-way ANOVA (unrelated)

Sources of variance	Sums of squares	Degrees of freedom	Mean squares	F ratios
Variable A (word length)	SS_A	df_A	$\dfrac{SS_A}{df_A}$	$\dfrac{MS_A}{MS_{error}}$
Variable B (presentation rate)	SS_B	df_B	$\dfrac{SS_B}{df_B}$	$\dfrac{MS_B}{MS_{error}}$
$A \times B$ (interaction)	SS_{AB}	df_{AB}	$\dfrac{SS_{AB}}{df_{AB}}$	$\dfrac{MS_{AB}}{MS_{error}}$
Error	SS_{error}	df_{error}	$\dfrac{SS_{error}}{df_{error}}$	
Total	SS_{tot}	df_{tot}		

presentation and more long words being recalled with a slow rate of presentation.

ANOVA sources of variance table

The 2×2 ANOVA sources of variance table shown in Table 15.6 is inevitably more complex than a one-way ANOVA. In a one-way design SS_{bet} represents all the predicted differences between conditions. In a 2×2 ANOVA SS_{bet} is split up between SS_A for variable A, SS_B for variable B and the possibility of an interaction between the two variables (SS_{AB}). Calculating the degrees of freedom is also more complicated (refer back to Table 15.2).

Rationale

As with one-way ANOVA we calculate sums of squares for each source of variance, in each case subtracting the same constant. Because SS_{bet} has been apportioned between the A, B and $A \times B$ variance we have to calculate these sums of squares separately. The F ratios for A, B and $A \times B$ represent the size of the variances due to variable A, variable B and the $A \times B$ interaction between the variables in relation to error variance.

Step-by-step instructions for calculating F

We include step-by-step instructions (see Box M) for anyone who does not have access to a computer.

Box M

Step-by-step instructions for calculating 2 × 2 *F* ratios (unrelated)

1 Note the following symbols (see Table 15.5):

$\sum T_a^2$ = sum of *A* squared totals $\qquad$ $\sum T_a^2 = 45^2 + 40^2$

$\sum T_b^2$ = sum of *B* squared totals $\qquad$ $\sum T_b^2 = 45^2 + 40^2$

$\sum T_{ab}^2$ = the sum of *AB* squared totals $\qquad$ $\sum T_{ab}^2 = 30^2 + 15^2 + 15^2 + 25^2$

$\qquad$ *n* = number of subjects in each condition $\qquad$ *n* = 4

$\qquad$ *a* = number of conditions for variable *A* $\qquad$ *a* = 2

$\qquad$ *b* = number of conditions for variable *B* $\qquad$ *b* = 2

$\qquad$ *N* = total number of scores $\qquad$ *N* = 16

$(\sum x)^2$ = grand total squared $\qquad$ $(\sum x)^2 = 85^2$

$\dfrac{(\sum x)^2}{N}$ = constant to be subtracted from all SS $\qquad$ $\dfrac{85^2}{16} = 451.5625$

$\sum x^2$ = sum of each individual score squared

2 Calculate SS_A

$$\frac{\sum T_a^2}{nb} - \frac{(\sum x)^2}{N}$$

$\qquad = \dfrac{45^2 + 40^2}{4 \times 2} - 451.5625$

$\qquad = 453.125 - 451.5625$

$\qquad = 1.5625$

3 Calculate SS_B

$$\frac{\sum T_b^2}{na} - \frac{(\sum x)^2}{N}$$

$\qquad = \dfrac{45^2 + 40^2}{4 \times 2} - 451.5625$

$\qquad = 453.125 - 451.5625$

$\qquad = 1.5625$

4 Calculate SS_{AB}

$$\frac{\sum T_{ab}^2}{n} - \frac{(\sum x)^2}{N} - SS_A - SS_B$$

Note that you have already calculated SS_A and SS_B and the constant.

$\qquad = \dfrac{0^2 + 15^2 + 15^2 + 25^2}{4}$

$\qquad - 451.5625 - 1.5625$

$\qquad - 1.5625$

$\qquad = 493.75 - 451.5625$

$\qquad - 1.5625 - 1.5625$

$\qquad = 39.0625$

5   Calculate SS_{tot}

$$\sum x^2 - \frac{(\sum x)^2}{N}$$

     $= 9^2 + 8^2 + 6^2 + 7^2$ plus all other individual scores squared

     $- 451.5625$

     $= 507 - 451.5625$

     $= 55.4375$

6   Calculate SS_{error}

$$SS_{tot} - SS_A - SS_B - SS_{AB}$$

     $= 55.4375 - 1.5625$

     $- 1.5625 - 39.0625$

     $= 13.25$

7   Calculate the degrees of freedom

     df_A = number of A conditions minus 1 $df_A = 2 - 1 = 1$

     df_B = number of B conditions minus 1 $df_B = 2 - 1 = 1$

     $df_{AB} = df_A \times df_B$ $df_{AB} = 1 \times 1 = 1$

     $df_{tot} = N - 1$ $df_{tot} = 16 - 1 = 15$

     $df_{error} = df_{tot} - df_A - df_B - df_{AB}$ $df_{error} = 15 - 1 - 1 - 1 = 12$

8   Divide each SS by df to obtain MS

$$MS_A = \frac{SS_A}{df_A}$$

     $MS_A = 1.5625$

$$MS_B = \frac{SS_B}{df_B}$$

     $MS_B = 1.5625$

$$MS_{AB} = \frac{SS_{AB}}{df_{AB}}$$

     $MS_{AB} = 39.0625$

$$MS_{error} = \frac{SS_{error}}{df_{error}}$$

     $MS_{error} = 1.104$

9   Calculate F ratios for MS_A, MS_B and MS_{AB} allocating the correct df to the F ratios

$$F \text{ ratio for } MS_A = \frac{MS_A}{MS_{error}}$$

     $F_{1,12} = 1.415$

$$F \text{ ratio for } MS_B = \frac{MS_B}{MS_{error}}$$

     $F_{1,12} = 1.415$

$$F \text{ ratio for } MS_{AB} = \frac{MS_{AB}}{MS_{error}}$$

     $F_{1,12} = 35.38$

10   The completed ANOVA table is shown in Table 15.7.

Table 15.7   Two-way ANOVA table (unrelated)

Sources of variance	Sums of squares	Degrees of freedom	Mean squares	F ratios
Variable A (word length)	1.5625	1	1.5625	$F_{1,12} = 1.415$
Variable B (presentation rate)	1.5625	1	1.5625	$F_{1,12} = 1.415$
A × B (interaction)	39.0625	1	39.0625	$F_{1,12} = 35.38$
Error	13.25	12	1.104	
Total	55.4375	15		

Looking up the significance of *F* in Table J

The computer package may have calculated the significance levels of the *F* ratios for you. But it would be a good idea for you to look up the *F* ratios yourself following the instructions given here. Start by locating the appropriate *df*. For all the *F* ratios in Table 15.7, $v_1 = 1$ and $v_2 = 12$. Since the calculated *F* ratios for variable *A* and variable *B* are smaller than the value of 4.75 for $F_{1,12}$ in Table J(1), neither the main effects of word length nor of presentation rate are significant. However, the calculated *F* ratio of 35.38 for the interaction $A \times B$ is larger than the value in Table J(1), and indeed larger than the values for $F_{1,12}$ in Tables J(2)–J(4), indicating that the interaction is significant ($p < 0.001$).

Output of computer packages

The output of a computer package will be in the form of an ANOVA table as shown in Table 15.7. You should look at this ANOVA table carefully to make sure that you understand the way in which the sums of squares have been divided by the degrees of freedom to produce mean squares and how the *F* ratios have been calculated and looked up in Table J.

Interpreting graphs

Many computer packages also provide a *graph* showing the data for each condition. The slopes of lines indicate whether the main effects or interactions appear significant. It is essential to check the labelling of these graphs so you can work out which conditions are being compared. The means for each of the four conditions in Table 15.5 have been calculated

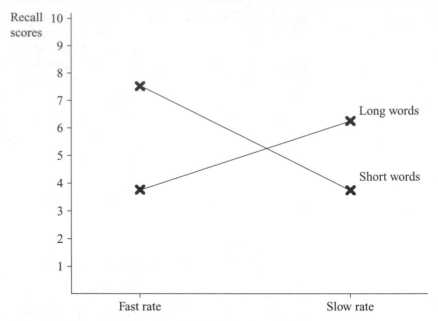

Figure 15.1   Graph for 2 × 2 ANOVA (unrelated)

in order to plot them on the graph in Figure 15.1. Look back to Table 15.5 to check that the means are the cell totals divided by the four subjects in each cell, e.g. 30 ÷ 4 = 7.5, and so on.

It is customary to plot the dependent variable, i.e. subjects' recall scores, up the vertical axis. It is often obvious which variable produced these scores but sometimes, as in this case, both variables are directly related to the scores. In the graph in Figure 15.1, the fast and slow presentation rates are plotted along the horizontal axis and the mean scores for long and short words are plotted against the recall scores on the vertical axis.

Conclusions

It is obvious from this graph that there is a strong interaction between word length and study period. This is borne out by the significant F ratio ($p < 0.001$). More long words were recalled at a slow rate of presentation and more short words at a fast presentation.

Can you think of a reason why this result was significant?

One possible reason might be that to memorize long words takes longer, therefore more words are remembered with a slow rate of presentation. More short words may originally be remembered but with a slow rate of presentation there is time for them to be forgotten. You can see from this discussion how essential it is to make sure which way round the significant interaction is from the means and a graph. It is all too easy to accept the output of a computer package without checking this out.

? Question 49 Look at the data in Table 15.8 showing a 2 × 3 table in which different subjects do each of the six conditions (unrelated).

Table 15.8 Data for 2 × 3 unrelated ANOVA

Variable B	Variable A		Totals B
	A_1	A_1	
B_1	7	2	
	9	1	
	6	2	
	22	5	27
B_2	6	3	
	6	3	
	5	2	
	17	8	25
B_3	3	5	
	1	6	
	1	4	
	5	15	20
Totals *A*	44	28	72

(a) Construct an ANOVA sources of variance table. Your table will be of the same form as in Table 15.7 (it makes no difference that you have three conditions for one variable until you come to the actual calculations). Calculate the degrees of freedom (*df*) for each source of variance. The *df* will be affected by the number of conditions and subjects for each variable. *Hint*: Look back at Table 15.2.

(b) Calculate the sums of squares, mean squares and *F* ratios for each source of variance.

(c) Are any of the *F* ratios significant?

Table 15.9   Recall scores for two variables (related)

| Subject | A_1 *(short words)* | | A_2 *(long words)* | |
	B_1 *(fast rate)*	B_2 *(slow rate)*	B_1 *(fast rate)*	B_2 *(slow rate)*
1	7	7	3	5
2	5	6	1	3
3	6	8	2	5
4	4	9	2	4
Means	5.5	7.75	2	4.25

15.3   Two-way ANOVA (related)

When to use

This analysis is used when *two variables* are tested with *two or more* conditions for each variable and the *same* subjects are used for all experimental conditions.

Sample data

Four subjects are given ten words to learn representing a combination of two levels of variable *A* (word length) and two levels of variable *B* (rate of presentation). Recall scores are shown in Table 15.9.

Hypothesis

The rate of presentation and the word length variables will have a significant effect on the dependent variable of recalled scores. Subjects will be able to recall more short words than long words and scores will be significantly higher with a slow rate of presentation. We also predict that there will be no interaction between the two variables *A* and *B*.

ANOVA sources of variance table (related)

The sources of variance table for a 2×2 related ANOVA is shown in Table 15.10. In a related ANOVA the differences between subjects across conditions can be treated as if they are a separate source of variance. So for the 2×2 related design the sources of variance table in Table 15.10

Table 15.10 Two-way ANOVA (related)

Sources of variance	Sums of squares	Degrees of freedom	Mean squares	F ratios
Variable A (word length)	SS_A	df_A	$\dfrac{SS_A}{df_A}$	$\dfrac{MS_A}{MS_{AS}}$
Variable B (presentation rate)	SS_B	df_B	$\dfrac{SS_B}{df_B}$	$\dfrac{MS_B}{MS_{BS}}$
S (subjects)	SS_S	df_S	$\dfrac{SS_S}{df_S}$	$\dfrac{MS_S}{MS_{ABS}}$
$A \times B$ (interaction)	SS_{AB}	df_{AB}	$\dfrac{SS_{AB}}{df_{AB}}$	$\dfrac{MS_{AB}}{MS_{ABS}}$
Error AS	SS_{AS}	df_{AS}	$\dfrac{SS_{AS}}{df_{AS}}$	
Error BS	SS_{BS}	df_{BS}	$\dfrac{SS_{BS}}{df_{BS}}$	
Error ABS	SS_{ABS}	df_{ABS}	$\dfrac{SS_{ABS}}{df_{ABS}}$	
Total	SS_{tot}	df_{tot}		

has to include not only the two variables A and B but also a third variable, subjects (S). The effect of this extra S variable on the calculations is quite dramatic, because now we have to take into account not only the interaction between the two variables ($A \times B$) but also the appropriate error variances of each of the variables separately, AS, BS and ABS, which represent in each case the individual differences between subjects *within* each of these conditions. You will see, therefore, in Table 15.10 that the F ratios for A, B and $A \times B$ include different error terms. To sum up, you can think of this design as a 2×2 design but with a third variable of the differences between individual subjects across all conditions. This is made possible by the fact that the same subjects are doing all the conditions, whereas in the unrelated two-way ANOVA each subject was performing under only one of the four conditions.

Rationale

The general method for calculating the sums of squares and deducting a constant is identical to the previous ANOVA calculations. The F ratios

Table 15.11   Summary tables for related data:

(a)   *AB* summary table

	A_1		A_2		*Totals B (T_b)*
B_1	7 5		3 1		
	6 4		2 2		
		22		8	30
B_2	7 6		5 3		
	8 9		5 4		
		30		17	47
Totals A (T_a)		52		25	77 Grand total

(b)   *AS* summary table

	A_1		A_2		*Totals S (T_s)*
S_1	7 7		3 5		
		14		8	22
S_2	5 6		1 3		
		11		4	15
S_3	6 8		2 5		
		14		7	21
S_4	4 9		2 4		
		13		6	19
Totals A (T_a)		52		25	77 Grand total

(c) *BS* summary table

	B_1		B_2		Totals S (T_s)
S_1	7	3	7	5	
		10		12	22
S_2	5	1	6	3	
		6		9	15
S_3	6	2	8	5	
		8		13	21
S_4	4	2	9	4	
		6		13	19
Totals B (T_b)		30		47	77 Grand total

for A, B, $A \times B$ represent the size of the variances due to experimental conditions and interactions in relation to error variance. To be significant the calculated value of the statistic F has to be *equal to* or *larger than* the critical values in Table J.

Preparing the data

When there are two related variables, it helps if we separate the scores and rearrange them into three tables showing the scores and totals for the *AB* conditions, the *AS* conditions and the *BS* conditions. In effect, this splits the data into one 2×2 table for the variables A and B (Table 15.11(a)) and two tables for $A \times$ subjects (Table 15.11(b)) and $B \times$ subjects (Table 15.11(c)). You will notice that each of the summary tables contains all the scores for each subject in Table 15.9 but in different combinations of conditions. You can check that all subjects' scores are included in each summary table by noting that the grand total of scores is the same for each table.

Step-by-step instruction for calculating *F* ratios

Once again we give the step-by-step instructions (Box N) for anyone who does not have access to a computer.

Box N

Step-by-step instructions for calculating 2×2 F ratios (related)

1   Note the following symbols
    (see Table 15.11):

$\sum T_a^2$ = sum of A squared $\sum T_a^2 = 52^2 + 25^2$
        totals Table 15.11 (a)

$\sum T_b^2$ = sum of B squared totals $\sum T_b^2 = 30^2 + 47^2$
        Table 15.11 (a)

$\sum T_s^2$ = sum of squared totals $\sum T_s^2 = 22^2 + 15^2 + 21^2 + 19^2$
        for each subject
        Table 15.11 (b)

$\sum T_{ab}^2$ = sum of AB squared $\sum T_{ab}^2 = 22^2 + 30^2 + 8^2 + 17^2$
        totals for individual
        cells in Table 15.11 (a)

$\sum T_{as}^2$ = sum of AS squared $\sum T_{as}^2 = 14^2 + 11^2 + 14^2 + 13^2 + 8^2 + 4^2$
        totals for individual $+ 7^2 + 6^2$
        cells in Table 15.11 (b)

$\sum T_{bs}^2$ = sum of BS squared $\sum T_{bs}^2 = 10^2 + 6^2 + 8^2 + 6^2 + 12^2 + 9^2$
        totals for the individual $+ 13^2 + 13^2$
        cells in Table 15.11 (c)

n = numbers of subjects $n = 4$

a = number of conditions $a = 2$
        for variable A

b = number of conditions $b = 2$
        for variable B

N = total number of scores $N = 16$

$(\sum x)^2$ = grand total squared $(\sum x)^2 = 77^2$

$\dfrac{(\sum x)^2}{N} = \begin{matrix} \text{constant to be} \\ \text{subtracted from all SS} \end{matrix}$ $= \dfrac{77^2}{16} = 370.5625$

$\sum x^2$ = sum of each individual
        score squared

2   Calculate SS_A $= \dfrac{52^2 + 25^2}{4 \times 2} - 370.5625$

$\dfrac{\sum T_a^2}{nb} - \dfrac{(\sum x)^2}{N}$ $= 416.125 - 370.5625$

$= 45.5625$

3 Calculate SS_B

$$\frac{\sum T_b^2}{na} - \frac{(\sum x)^2}{N}$$

$= \dfrac{30^2 + 47^2}{4 \times 2} - 370.5625$

$= 388.625 - 370.5625$

$= 18.0625$

4 Calculate SS_S

$$\frac{\sum T_s^2}{ab} - \frac{(\sum x)^2}{N}$$

$= \dfrac{22^2 + 15^2 + 21^2 + 19^2}{4} - 370.5625$

$= 377.75 - 370.5625$

$= 7.1875$

5 Calculate SS_{AB}

$$\frac{\sum T_{ab}^2}{n} - \frac{(\sum x)^2}{N} - SS_A - SS_B$$

$= \dfrac{22^2 + 30^2 + 8^2 + 17^2}{4}$

$\quad - 370.5625 - 45.5625 - 18.0625$

$= 434.25 - 370.5625 - 45.5625 - 18.0625$

$= 0.0625$

6 Calculate SS_{AS}

$$\frac{\sum T_{as}^2}{b} - \frac{(\sum x)^2}{N} - SS_A - SS_S$$

$= \dfrac{14^2 + 11^2 + 14^2 + 13^2 + 8^2 + 4^2 + 7^2 + 6^2}{2}$

$\quad - 370.5625 - 45.5625 - 7.1875$

$= 423.5 - 370.5625 - 45.5625 - 7.1875$

$= 0.1875$

7 Calculate SS_{BS}

$$\frac{\sum T_{bs}^2}{a} - \frac{(\sum x)^2}{N} - SS_B - SS_S$$

$= \dfrac{10^2 + 6^2 + 8^2 + 6^2 + 12^2 + 9^2 + 13^2 + 13^2}{2}$

$\quad - 370.5625 - 18.0625 - 7.1875$

$= 399.5 - 370.5625 - 18.0625 - 7.1875$

$= 3.6875$

8 Calculate SS_{tot}

$$\sum x^2 - \frac{(\sum x)^2}{N}$$

$= 7^2 + 5^2 + 6^2 + 4^2$ plus all other individual scores squared $- 370.5625$

$= 449 - 370.5625$

$= 78.4375$

9   Calculate SS_{ABS}

$SS_{tot} - SS_A - SS_B - SS_S$ $= 78.4375 - 45.5625 - 18.0625 - 7.1875$
$- SS_{AB} - SS_{AS} - SS_{BS}$ $- 0.0625 - 0.1875 - 3.6875$

                                    $= 3.6875$

10   Calculate the degrees of freedom

$$df_A = 2 - 1 = 1$$
$$df_B = 2 - 1 = 1$$
$$df_S = 4 - 1 = 3$$
$$df_{AB} = 1 \times 1 = 1$$
$$df_{AS} = 1 \times 3 = 3$$
$$df_{BS} = 1 \times 3 = 3$$
$$df_{ABS} = 1 \times 1 \times 3 = 3$$
$$df_{tot} = 16 - 1 = 15$$

11   Divide each SS by df to obtain MS

$$MS_A = 45.5625$$
$$MS_B = 18.0625$$
$$MS_S = 2.3958$$
$$MS_{AB} = 0.0625$$
$$MS_{AS} = 0.0625$$
$$MS_{BS} = 1.229$$
$$MS_{ABS} = 1.229$$

12   Calculate F ratios allocating correct df to each F ratio

F ratio for $MS_A = \dfrac{MS_A}{MS_{AS}}$ $F_{1,3} = 729$

F ratio for $MS_B = \dfrac{MS_B}{MS_{BS}}$ $F_{1,3} = 14.7$

F ratio for $MS_S = \dfrac{MS_S}{MS_{ABS}}$ $F_{3,3} = 1.95$

F ratio for $MS_{AB} = \dfrac{MS_{AB}}{MS_{ABS}}$ $F_{1,3} = 0.051$

13   The completed ANOVA table is shown in Table 15.12.

Table 15.12   Two-way ANOVA table (related)

Sources of variance	Sums of squares	Degrees of freedom	Mean squares	F ratios
Variable A (word length)	45.5625	1	45.5625	$F_{1,3} = 729$
Variable B (presentation rate)	18.0625	1	18.0625	$F_{1,3} = 14.7$
S (subjects)	7.1875	3	2.3958	$F_{3,3} = 1.95$
$A \times B$ (interaction)	0.0625	1	0.0625	$F_{1,3} = 0.051$
Error AS	0.1875	3	0.0625	
Error BS	3.6875	3	1.229	
Error ABS	3.6875	3	1.229	
Total	78.4375	15		

Looking up the significance of F in Table J

In Table J(4) the value for $F_{1,3}$ is 167 at the $p < 0.001$ level of significance. Since the calculated value of F for variable A is 729, the predicted
effect of word length on recall scores is significant at this level, i.e. more
short words are recalled than long words ($p < 0.001$). In Table J(1) the
value for $F_{1,3}$ is 10.13 at the $p < 0.05$ level of significance. Since the
calculated value of F for variable B is 14.7 the effect of presentation rate
on recall scores is significant ($p < 0.05$).

Not surprisingly, the calculated value for the interaction $A \times B$, $F_{1,3} =$
0.051, is not significant at any of the levels given in Tables J(1)–J(4), since
it is smaller than any of the values for $F_{1,3}$. It is usual also to check the F
value for the subjects variance in case a high proportion of the variance is
caused by differences between subjects. The observed value of $F_{3,3} = 1.95$
is not significant.

Inputs to computer packages

It will help to draw up the three tables in Table 15.11 so that you understand which totals you are inputting to the computer. You will also need
to indicate which scores come from how many subjects in each condition.

Outputs of computer packages

The output will be in the form of an ANOVA table as shown in Table 15.12.
The other output of the computer package is likely to be *graphs* of the means

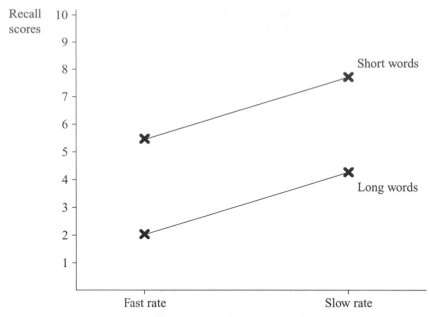

Figure 15.2   Graph of 2×2 ANOVA (related)

to show the direction of these effects, as in Figure 15.2. In Figure 15.2, using the means from Table 15.9, the recall scores are plotted up the vertical axis, fast and short presentation rates along the horizontal axis and the short and long words are plotted as data points against the recall scores.

Remember that it is essential to refer back to the means when plotting graphs and interpreting results. In this case, only the main effects of word length ($p < 0.001$) and presentation rate ($p < 0.05$) are significant. It is only from looking at the means in Table 15.9 and the graph in Figure 15.2 that it is clear that more short words are recalled than long words and that both kinds of words are recalled better with a slow rate of presentation. The parallel slopes in Figure 15.2 demonstrate that there is no interaction between the two variables.

Question 50 (a) Draw a second graph to display the same means from Table 15.9. This time plot recall scores up the vertical axis and place short words and long words along the horizontal axis. Plot the means for long and slow presentation rates as data points, joined up by lines.

(b) What conclusions can be drawn from this graph?

(c) Are these results consistent with the results found using different subjects in Section 15.2?

Conclusions

As predicted, slow presentation rates produced better recall scores than fast presentation rates ($p < 0.05$) and short words were easier to recall than long words ($p < 0.001$). The interaction between these two effects was not significant.

15.4   Two-way ANOVA (mixed)

When to use

This mixed design is included as an example of the kinds of two-way ANOVA designs which experimenters often use. It is called a **mixed design** because one variable is *related* (all subjects do all conditions) while the other variable is *unrelated* (different subjects do each of the conditions).

Sample data

Nine subjects are allocated in groups of three to each of the three conditions for variable *A* (word length). All subjects are tested under *all* three conditions for variable *B* (rate of presentation). In other words, three subjects are presented with each of the lists of words: S_1, S_2 and S_3 with short words, S_4, S_5, S_6 with medium words, S_7, S_8, S_9 with long words. But *all* the subjects are presented with lists at a fast rate, at a medium rate and at a slow rate. The data is shown in Table 15.13.

This design is a two-way 3×3 design, because it has *two* variables, each with *three* conditions. The word length conditions are done by *different* subjects, i.e. *between* subjects and the presentation rate conditions are done by the *same* subjects (*within* subjects). This is why it is called a mixed design.

Hypothesis

The hypothesis is that there will be an interaction between presentation rate and word length. More short words will be recalled at faster rates of presentation and more long words at slower presentation rates.

ANOVA sources of variance table (mixed)

The sources of variance ANOVA table for a mixed design is complicated by the calculation of different error terms for variable *A* (*AS*) and variable *B* ($B \times AS$) as shown in Table 15.14. This is because it is only possible to calculate subject variance for variable *B*.

Table 15.13   Recall scores for two variables (mixed)

		B_1 (fast rate)		B_2 (medium rate)		B_3 (slow rate)		Totals S (T_s)	Totals A (T_a)
A_1 (short words)	S_1	8		4		3		15	
	S_2	7		4		4		15	
	S_3	7		5		2		14	
			22		13		9		44
A_2 (medium length words)	S_4	4		4		3		11	
	S_5	6		7		5		18	
	S_6	7		5		6		18	
			17		16		14		47
A_3 (long words)	S_7	2		4		6		12	
	S_8	4		6		7		17	
	S_9	3		6		5		14	
			9		16		18		43
Totals B (T_b)		48		45		41		134 Grand total	134 Grand total

Table 15.14   Two-way ANOVA (mixed)

Sources of variance	Sums of squares	Degrees of freedom	Mean squares	F ratios
Variable A (word length)	SS_A	df_A	$\dfrac{SS_A}{df_A}$	$\dfrac{MS_A}{MS_{AS}}$
Error AS	SS_{AS}	df_{AS}	$\dfrac{SS_{AS}}{df_{AS}}$	
Variable B (presentation rate)	SS_B	df_B	$\dfrac{SS_B}{df_B}$	$\dfrac{MS_B}{MS_{B \times AS}}$
$A \times B$ (interaction)	SS_{AB}	df_{AB}	$\dfrac{SS_{AB}}{df_{AB}}$	$\dfrac{MS_{AB}}{MS_{B \times AS}}$
Error $B \times AS$	$SS_{B \times AS}$	$df_{B \times AS}$	$\dfrac{SS_{B \times AS}}{df_{B \times AS}}$	
Total	SS_{tot}	df_{tot}		

Rationale

The general method for calculating sums of squares for each source of variance is the same as for the simpler ANOVAs, squaring the appropriate totals and subtracting a *constant*. As with the two-way related ANOVA, a special error variance has to be calculated for each variable. The only difference with the mixed case is that, since it is only the variable *B* conditions which are being done by all subjects, it is not possible to calculate a variance due to subjects' overall performance across both variables.

The *F* ratios for *A*, *B*, *A* × *B* represent the size of the variance due to experimental conditions and interactions in relation to error variance. To be significant the calculated value of the statistic *F* has to be *equal to* or *larger than* the critical values in Table J.

Preparing the data

In order to calculate a mixed ANOVA the totals and grand total need to be calculated as shown in Table 15.13.

Step-by-step instructions for calculating *F* ratios

We are assuming that you will be using a computer package for this analysis. In Box O (overleaf) we give the formulae for each step but not the detailed calculations. If you are doing this by hand using a calculator you can look back to the step-by-step instructions for the two-way related and unrelated ANOVAs to check what all the symbols mean (see Sections 15.2 and 15.3). Our calculations are shown in Table 15.15.

Table 15.15 Two-way ANOVA table (mixed)

Sources of variance	Sums of squares	Degrees of freedom	Mean squares	F ratios
Variable *A* (word length)	0.97	2	0.485	$F_{2,6} = 0.189$
Error *AS*	15.33	6	2.555	
Variable *B* (presentation rate)	2.75	2	1.375	$F_{2,12} = 1.903$
A × *B* (interaction)	43.25	4	10.8125	$F_{4,12} = 14.965$
Error *B* × *AS*	8.67	12	0.7225	
Total	70.97	26		

■ **Box O**

Step-by-step instructions for calculating F ratios (mixed)

Calculate SS using the following formulae
(see Table 15.13).

Note that n = number of subjects in each A $n = 3$
condition.

a and b are the number of conditions for $a = 3$
the A and B variables. $b = 3$

N = total number of subjects across A and $N = 27$
B conditions.

1   Calculate SS_A from the formula $\dfrac{\sum T_a^2}{nb} - \dfrac{(\sum x)^2}{N}$

2   Calculate SS_{AS} from the formula $\dfrac{\sum T_s^2}{b} - \dfrac{(\sum x)^2}{N} - SS_A$

3   Calculate SS_B from the formula $\dfrac{\sum T_b^2}{na} - \dfrac{(\sum x)^2}{N}$

4   Calculate SS_{AB} from the formula $\dfrac{\sum T_{ab}^2}{n} - \dfrac{(\sum x)^2}{N} - SS_A - SS_B$

5   Calculate SS_{tot} from the formula $\sum x^2 - \dfrac{(\sum x)^2}{N}$

6   Calculate $SS_{B \times AS}$ from the formula $SS_{tot} - SS_A - SS_{AS} - SS_B - SS_{AB}$

7   Calculate the degrees of freedom $df_A = 3 - 1 = 2$
     $df_B = 3 - 1 = 2$
     $df_{AB} = 2 \times 2 = 4$
     $df_{AS} = 2 \times 3 = 6$
     $df_{B \times AS} = 2 \times 6 = 12$
     $df_{tot} = 27 - 1 = 26$

8   Divide each SS by the df to obtain MS

9   Calculate F ratios allocating correct df

$$F_{2,6}\ MS_A = \frac{MS_A}{MS_{AS}}$$

$$F_{2,12}\ MS_B = \frac{MS_B}{MS_{B \times AS}}$$

$$F_{4,12}\ MS_{AB} = \frac{MS_{AB}}{MS_{B \times AS}}$$

10   The completed ANOVA table is shown in
Table 15.15.

Looking up the significance of *F* ratios in Table J

Once you have calculated the *F* ratios using either a computer package or a calculator, look them up in the normal way in Table J, taking into account the appropriate degrees of freedom. Neither the *F* ratios for variable *A* nor variable *B* are significant at df 2, 6 and df 2, 12 respectively. The calculated value of 14.965 for the interaction is larger than the value for $F_{4,12}$ in Table J(4) and so is significant ($p < 0.001$).

Conclusions

If you look at the subtotals for each cell in Table 15.13 you can see that, as predicted, recall scores are highest for short words at faster rates of presentation and for long words at slower rates of presentation.

15.5   Comparisons between individual conditions

One of the drawbacks of ANOVA is that it only analyses whether there are *overall* differences between conditions. With the 2 × 2 ANOVA designs discussed in this chapter, the total variance is accounted for by the main effects, the interactions and error variances. But when there are *three* conditions for a single variable there may be more ambiguity. When *one-way ANOVA* was introduced in Chapter 13 for dealing with three or more conditions, it was pointed out that ANOVA could only test whether there were overall differences. Suppose, for instance, there are three conditions, the effects of fast, medium or slow rates of presentation on recall of lists of words. ANOVA can decide whether there are overall differences between these conditions. But it cannot test which particular conditions have contributed to these differences. From this point of view a one-way ANOVA is a two-tailed test because it does not test predictions in a specific direction.

One possibility is that there may be a trend, with fast presentation producing the worst recall, medium rate medium recall, slow rates the best recall. But there are other possibilities of how the data may turn out. Perhaps the fast rate produces least recall but there is no difference between medium and slow rates. ANOVA might still show overall differences. One way of investigating this is to draw a graph of the means for each condition, as shown in Figures 15.3 and 15.4.

The scores in Figure 15.3 indicate that there is likely to be a trend between *A*, *B* and *C*. It would be possible to test this using a non-parametric trend test.

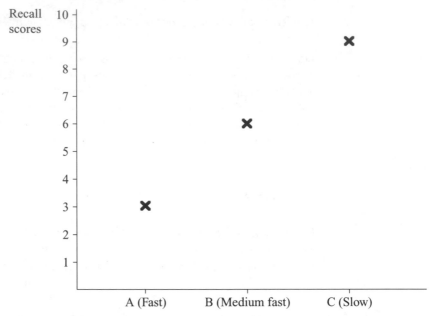

Figure 15.3   Graph showing trend between three conditions

? Question 51 If the scores in Figure 15.3 came from the same subjects in a related design, what would be the appropriate non-parametric trend test?

In Figure 15.4, it is clear that most of the differences are between the fast rate and the slow/medium rates. The graph shows that there is not much difference between scores in the *B* (slow) and *C* (medium) rates. The variability in subjects' scores is due to the difference between the low mean recall score for the fast rate (*A*) and higher mean scores for the other two rates of presentation (*C* and *B*).

The basic method for making **comparisons between conditions** is the *t* test. This is because the aim is to test whether there is a difference between *A* and *B*, and between *A* and *C*, but no difference between *B* and *C*. The comparisons are being made between *pairs* of conditions and the *t* test is the appropriate test for testing two conditions.

There is one important factor that has to be taken into account when making comparisons between pairs of conditions. Basically the researcher is being allowed to test other predictions using the same data. The original hypothesis was that there would be *overall* differences in no particular

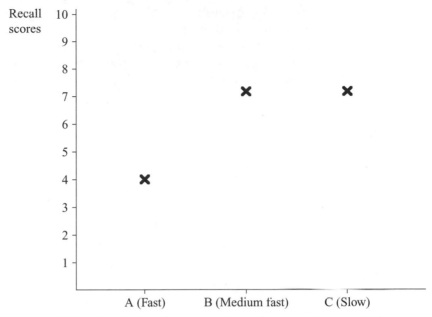

Figure 15.4 Graph showing comparisons between three conditions

direction. Now the researcher is making a new hypothesis that there will be differences in a particular direction, with the fast presentation rate producing less recall than the medium and slow rates of presentation. This mention of hypotheses about overall differences and hypotheses predicting differences in a particular direction should remind you of differences between *two-tailed* and *one-tailed* hypotheses.

The crucial feature is that a one-tailed hypothesis makes only one prediction and a two-tailed hypothesis makes two predictions, one in each direction. The levels of significance are different for one-tailed and two-tailed hypotheses. The fact that more predictions are being made to test comparisons means that attention must be paid to the increased probability of obtaining a level of significance for at least some of these comparisons when they are really due to random variability.

There is a test called the **Tukey test** which analyses the possibilities of comparisons between specific pairs of conditions. It is especially designed to take account of the number of extra predicted differences which are being made. Because of this the Tukey test is known as Tukey (HSD), which stands for 'Honestly Significant Difference'.

The Tukey test is not particularly difficult to calculate because it uses the *t* tests you already know and uses the variance calculated in the ANOVA as error variance. Rather than adding another test to this book, you will be able to look up the Tukey test in more advanced books like Clark-Carter (1977) and Dunbar (1998). The Tukey test is also commonly available in computerized statistical packages to carry out extra tests on ANOVA data. But there is a word of warning before any comparisons are tested. *The absolutely crucial point is that it is never permissible to make any further comparisons unless the original ANOVA shows significant overall differences in the first place.*

Epilogue

Fifteen chapters – and 15 statistical tests – further on, what might our researcher and sceptical teacher think now? In the Prologue they were talking about the efficiency of psychological research as a means of studying people's behaviour.

Sceptical teacher: I think you have now convinced me that it is possible to measure the reading performance of children who are given a reading scheme and to use a statistical test to decide whether that performance is *significantly* different from that of other children. I also see how important it is to try and eliminate other irrelevant variables which might be affecting their behaviour.

Researcher: It is kind of you to say so. But I would feel somewhat uneasy if I did not draw your attention to some problems concerning the *interpretation* of the results from an experiment.

Sceptic: You mean what is the 'real' significance of statistically significant results?

Researcher: You remember that accepting a result as being significant at a particular significance level means that there is a very small probability, say 1 per cent or 5 per cent, that the results might have occurred by a random combination of irrelevant variables. But, of course, you can never be certain that this random event did *not* occur. In fact, even a significant level of $p < 0.001$ means that there is a 1 in 1000 probability that it might have been a chance result as stated by the null hypothesis.

Sceptic: Is there any way I can guard against this?

Researcher: I am afraid not. Because you can never be 100 per cent certain whether it is the experimental or the null hypothesis which is true, there is always a risk that you might be drawing the wrong conclusions from an experiment. One error you might make is to *reject* the null hypothesis when it *is* in fact true. This is known as a *Type I error*. You can think of this as an optimistic error, because you are accepting that your results are significant when they are in fact random, since it is the null hypothesis which is true. Another error you might make is to *accept* the null hypothesis when it is *not* in fact true. This is known as a *Type II error*. You can think of this as a pessimistic error because in this case you are accepting that the results are due to random fluctuations in performance when they are really due to the effects predicted by the experimental hypothesis.

Sceptic: I'm not sure I follow your reasoning here. Are you saying that whatever significance level I accept, I run the risk of making an error?

Researcher: Just think, if one experimenter sets a significance level of $p < 0.01$ and another is prepared to accept a significance level of $p < 0.05$, which of the two is more likely to make a Type II error?

Sceptic: The experimenter who chooses a $p < 0.01$ significance level is more likely to make a pessimistic Type II error, and the experimenter who chooses a $p < 0.05$ significance level is more likely to make an optimistic Type I error. To see why, suppose both experimenters found that their results were significant at $p < 0.02$. The first experimenter would have to accept that the results are not significant because $p < 0.02$ is a higher probability than $p < 0.01$. The second experimenter would accept the results as being significant because $p < 0.02$ is a lower probability than $p < 0.05$. So from the very same results the first experimenter would pessimistically accept the null hypothesis, whereas the second experimenter would optimistically claim significant results although there is a 2 per cent chance that they were not significant at all.

Researcher: Well, I can't help wishing you were in my class of psychology students! The only point to remember is that neither experimenter is 'right' or 'wrong'. The first more cautious experimenter might, for instance, decide that the results of a drug test are not significant and so deprive patients of a drug that has a sporting chance of being beneficial.

Sceptic: But, allowing for this probability angle, can I at least accept that the results of an experiment are due to the variables manipulated by the experimenter?

Researcher: Naturally, I'd like to say yes to this one. But it is not really possible to claim that all possible irrelevant variables have been accounted for. I shall give you just one example to show how very difficult it is to be sure that any result is due to the independent variable the experimenter is interested in. Research showed that less of a particular hormone was found in the urine of schizophrenics than in a group of control subjects. This led to a lot of speculation about lack of these hormones as the cause of schizophrenia. No one had thought of investigating the hospital diet of the schizophrenics. When control subjects were fed the same diet they too produced hormone-deficient urine.

Sceptic: And I've just thought of another worry. I seem to remember having read that most experiments investigating psychological processes have been carried out using American university students. If this is true, how can you claim that experimental results are true of the human population in general?

Researcher: You have a point there. It has been said that all you learn from many experiments is how students react when asked to do things by their lecturers. Psychologists have become more aware of this problem. Especially in the field of personality and educational research much more effort has gone into making sure that tests of IQ or whatever have been validated by testing a sample which is truly representative of the population at large. Another area in which sampling is obviously very important is surveys into people's attitude or opinions. It is not much use quoting the results of an opinion poll or the market demand for a product if the sample of people questioned does not even know the product exists.

Sceptic: But what about individual differences? Surely people are so different that you can't draw any conclusions about general laws of behaviour that apply to all human beings?

Researcher: This is one of the really tricky questions for psychologists. In one sense every person is unique. On the other hand, if every human being had to be tested individually, it would be impossible to make any general statements about the way in which people learn or remember things or the likely effects of introducing a new method for teaching reading.

Sceptic: I see that. But I still can't help feeling that a lot of the experiments described in earlier chapters seem to be far removed from real-life behaviour. Can we really learn anything about everyday memory by asking students to remember lists of words?

Researcher: The question of whether experiments reflect real life has been formulated as the need for *ecological validity* and it is a perennial problem for psychological research. It is almost an automatic reflex on the part of an experimenter to standardize the conditions of an experiment so that subjects will be likely to behave in a uniform fashion. The more opportunities subjects have for misinterpreting instructions, interacting in idiosyncratic ways with the experimenter, or reacting to irrelevant variables in the situation, the more general variability there will be in their performance. Nevertheless, it is a good thing for experimenters to remember that, perhaps unfortunately for them – but luckily for the rest of us – variety is the spice of life. Even in the most standardized conditions human beings still tend to react in all sorts of ways.

Sceptic: What should a psychologist do? Is there a solution?

Researcher: There is no one correct solution. All these 'strengths' and 'weaknesses' represent a trade-off between the precision that comes from experimental controls and a loss of 'real-life' richness. It all depends on the purpose of an experiment, the conditions under which it is going to be carried out, the conclusions which will be drawn from it, and the stage of the research programme. Sometimes it is necessary to rely on intuitive accounts of people's feelings. These may in turn suggest theories about human nature which can be put to a more precise experimental test. But, whatever the aims of a research project, it is obvious that awareness of possible alternative explanations and the various methods of controlling for them are essential skills for any psychologist.

Sceptic: My reactions to all this are still rather muddled. What *are* the advantages and disadvantages of doing *experiments* with human beings?

Researcher: That's the kind of thing I can show best by producing yet another 'Progress Box'.

Sceptic: Shall we agree, then, that the lot of a psychological researcher is a hard one, but that the attempt to develop methods for the systematic study of human beings is a rewarding challenge?

Progress box thirteen

Advantages and disadvantages of experiments

Advantages	*Disadvantages*
• Formulation of an experimental hypothesis which predicts a precise relationship between variables	• It is not always possible to formulate a precise hypothesis particularly at the exploratory stage of a research programme
• Manipulating an independent variable to show its effect on a dependent variable	• There are situations when it is not practically or ethically possible to manipulate variables
• Collection of objective, quantitative data which can be statistically analysed to see whether it supports the experimental hypothesis	• The psychologist may ignore observational and intuitive evidence which may throw light on human behaviour
• Elimination of alternative explanations by eliminating irrelevant variables	• Control and standardization may result in artificial experimental situations that have no bearing on real-life behaviour

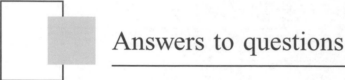

Answers to questions

Question 1

(a) The independent variable is whether people are given the illustrated text or the text without illustrations.
(b) The dependent variable is how long it takes people to read the texts.
(c) The experimental hypothesis predicts that people will take less time to read the illustrated text than the non-illustrated text.
(d) The null hypothesis is that the time people take to read a text is due, not to whether it is illustrated or not, but to random fluctations in people's performance.

Question 2

(a) The experimental hypothesis would predict that more common words will be recalled than rare words. Note that the theory is that common words are more easily accessed in memory. But the experimental hypothesis has to state the outcome of the experiment, which will be testing the number of words recalled.
(b) The null hypothesis predicts that the recall scores will be caused by random fluctuations in people's performance.

(c) *Experimental condition 1*
    Learning common words
    Experimental condition 2
    Learning rare words

(d) The dependent variable is the recall scores.
(e) Yes. The experimental hypothesis predicted higher recall scores for common words.

Question 3

(a) *Experimental condition 1*
    Learning very common words
    Experimental condition 2
    Learning less common words
    Experimental condition 3
    Learning very rare words

(b) The experimental hypothesis might predict that subjects will recall more very common words than less common words and more less common words than very rare words.

Question 4

(a) Four subjects recalled 5 ideas.
(b) Four subjects recalled 4 ideas and only two subjects recalled 7 ideas.
(c) No, because there is no square for 0 ideas.
(d) One subject recalled all 10 ideas.
(e) Twenty subjects, as represented by the 20 squares in Figure 3.1, representing ten subjects in condition 1 plus ten subjects in condition 2 in Table 3.1.

Question 5

(a) Three subjects.
(b) One subject.
(c) The subjects in condition 1 recalled more ideas, as shown by the differences in the means in Table 3.1.
(d) Six subjects in condition 2 had a higher recall score than the subject in condition 1 who recalled only three ideas.

Question 6

(a) The correct answer is 1 in 1000, i.e. ($p < 0.001$).
(b) $p < 0.001$ (1 in 1000) represents the greatest level of significance since there is only a 0.1 per cent probability that the results of the experiment might have occurred randomly. This is less probable than $p < 0.01$ which represents a 1 per cent probability, and $p < 0.05$ which represents a 5 per cent probability.

Question 7

(a) The means are:

    Condition 1   15 (60 divided by 4)
    Condition 2   7.5 (30 divided by 4)

Because the same scores are presented in Tables 5.1 and 5.2, the means are the same for both tables. Check this for yourself.

(b) The scores in Table 5.1 are *related* because the pairs of scores in condition 1 and condition 2 come from the same subjects. In contrast, the scores in Table 5.2 come from different subjects and so are independent, hence *unrelated*.

Question 8

Table A.1   Ranks (Question 8)

Scores	Ranks
4	4.5
8	7
3	2.5
3	2.5
1	1
7	6
4	4.5

Notice that the two tied scores of 3 are assigned the average of ranks 2 and 3, which is 2.5. The two tied ranks of 4 are assigned the average of the next two available ranks 4 and 5, which is 4.5.

Question 9

Table A.2   Overall ranks (Question 9)

Condition 1		Condition 2	
Scores	Ranks	Scores	Ranks
1	1	3	3
4	4.5	4	4.5
6	7	5	6
2	2	7	8

Note that overall ranks have been assigned *across conditions*, for example, the rank of 4.5 has been assigned to the tied scores of 4, one in condition 1 and one in condition 2.

Question 10

(a) The 0 score for subject 4 in condition 1 is treated as a low score and compared with the same subject's score for condition 2 to give a difference of −5.

(b) The two 0 scores for subject 8 result in a *nil* difference in favour of either condition, as does the tie between the two scores of 4 for subject 5.

(c) As a consequence of the two ties, a total of eight ranks are available for assignment to the eight other differences. In this case, the two largest differences of +5 and −5 are themselves tied and so are assigned the average of ranks 7 and 8, i.e. 7.5. Note that the differences are ranked ignoring plus and minus signs.

Question 11

	Condition 1	Condition 2
(a) Means	3.25	4.75
(b) Rank totals	14.5	21.5

(c) Both the mean scores and the rank totals are higher for condition 2 than for condition 1. This is not surprising because the means reflect the differences in scores. The ranks also reflect the scores because the ranks are assigned to scores from lowest to highest, resulting in more high ranks for condition 2.

Question 12

	Condition 1	Condition 2
(a) Means	3.0	3.5

(b) The ranked differences add up to 36.

Note that the two ties for subjects 5 and 8 are ignored so the rank total is calculated from the eight ranked differences.

Question 13

The experimental hypothesis is one-tailed because the researcher made a prediction in one direction, that more words would be recalled in the music condition. A two-tailed hypothesis would have stated that music will make a difference to recall scores but in either direction, with more or fewer words being recalled in the music or silence conditions.

Question 14

The significance level of $p < 0.025$ means that the probability of a random result is 25 in 1000. This is a lower probability, and therefore more significant, than $p < 0.05$ (5 in 100). But $p < 0.001$ represents an even lower probability of 1 in 1000 and would therefore be more significant than $p < 0.025$.

If you are puzzled by any of this answer go back and reread Chapter 3, Section 3.3, about levels of significance.

Question 15

(a) The means are shown in Table A.3.
(b) Refer back to Table 6.1. The blank columns are completed in Table A.3. Because $(-)3$ is the smaller rank total $W = 3$.
$N = 8 - 1$ tie $= 7$.
In Table A, looking along the $N = 7$ row the calculated $W = 3$ is smaller than 4 but larger than 2. So the one-tailed hypothesis that texts with short sentences will be easier to comprehend is supported ($p < 0.05$).
(c) It would be essential to give half the subjects the simple text first followed by the complex text and the other half of the subjects in the reverse order, thus counterbalancing any order effects.

Table A.3 Wilcoxon test (Question 15)

	Scores (1)	Scores (2)	d	Ranks of d	Signed ranks (plus)	Signed ranks (minus)
	7	8	−1	−1		−1
	10	6	+4	+4.5	+4.5	
	13	4	+9	+7	+7	
	8	4	+4	+4.5	+4.5	
	7	7	0	(tie)	−	
	8	10	−2	−2		−2
	6	3	+3	+3	+3	
	10	3	+7	+6	+6	
Means	8.63	5.63		Rank totals	(+)25	(−)3

Question 16

In a related design subjects who were given the title first would not be able to forget the title when they were doing the no title condition. The only way to avoid this would be to use two different texts so that each subject would see one text with a title and a different text with no title. It is very difficult to equate two texts to ensure that they are of equal difficulty. If one text is easier to recall the results might be due to this irrelevant variable rather than the intended independent variable of title or no title. So it is better to use the same text and give one group of subjects a title and a different group of subjects no title in an unrelated design.

Question 17

I hope you can see that this is a nonsensical question. If each subject produces a pair of scores in each condition, there must be the same number of scores as there are subjects. So there must always be the same number of subjects in each condition in a related design.

Question 18

(a) The experiment was an unrelated design with different groups of subjects doing each condition. This is why the Mann–Whitney is the appropriate test.

	Condition 1	*Condition 2*
(b) Means	13.22	14.63

Note that there are different numbers of subjects in each group, so the totals have to be divided by these different numbers to calculate the means.

(c) One-tailed, because the experimenter predicted that the subjects in the group with left-hand presentation of words (condition 2) would recognize more words.

(d) The overall ranks of scores across both conditions and the rank totals are shown in Table A.4.

(e) In Table B(4) the calculated value of $U = 25$ for $n_1 = 9$, $n_2 = 8$ is larger than the required value of 18 for a $p < 0.05$ (one-tailed) level of significance.

Remember that for a value of U to be significant is has to be *equal to* or *less than* the values in Table B. So this value of U is not significant.

Note: If you got a different answer for the value of U, it may have been because you forgot to rank all the scores as a single set of overall scores across conditions, not for each condition separately. You may also have forgotten to work out U in the formula $U^1 = n_1 n_2 - U$ to check whether U or U^1 is the smaller value for U.

(f) Because the differences are not significant even at $p < 0.05$, the null hypothesis cannot be rejected. Consequently, the results cannot be interpreted as supporting the experimental hypothesis that more words would be recognized with left-hand presentation.

Table A.4 Mann–Whitney test (Question 18)

Scores (1)	*Overall ranks (rank 1)*	*Scores (2)*	*Overall ranks (rank 2)*
17	15	18	17
13	8	15	10.5
12	5.5	17	15
16	12.5	13	8
10	1.5	11	3.5
15	10.5	16	12.5
11	3.5	10	1.5
13	8	17	15
12	5.5		
	$T_1 = 70$ $(n_1 = 9)$		$T_2 = 83$ $(n_2 = 8)$

$$U = 9 \times 8 + \frac{9 \times 10}{2} - 70 = 72 + 45 - 70 = 47$$

$$U^1 = 9 \times 8 - 47 = 25$$

U is the smaller value of 25

Question 19

The illustrations were presented in different orders because the same children were being shown all three illustrations. If they had all been shown illustration A first and illustration C last their ratings might have been affected by being impressed by the first or last illustration rather than the intended variable of comparing the three illustrations regardless of order. This is why it is so important to counterbalance orders of presentation in a related design (see Chapter 2, Section 2.4).

Question 20

	Condition 1	Condition 2	Condition 3
(a)	3.6	6.6	7

(b) The independent variable is the colour in which the prose passages were printed. The dependent variable is the number of ideas recalled from each passage.

(c) The Friedman test for related designs is appropriate because the *same* five subjects read all *three* prose passages.

(d) Refer back to Table 7.1. Remember to rank *horizontally* across the three conditions for each subject before adding the rank totals to enter in the Box C step-by-step instructions (see Table A.5).

(e) In Table C(1), the calculated $\chi_r^2 = 6.7$ for $N = 5$ is larger than the value of 6.4 for $p < 0.039$ which is less probable than $p < 0.05$. So the Friedman test has demonstrated that there are overall differences between the conditions ($p < 0.05$). It would be necessary to use Page's L trend test to test for a trend.

Table A.5 Friedman test (Question 20)

Scores (1)	Ranks	Scores (2)	Ranks	Scores (3)	Ranks
4	1	5	2	6	3
2	1	7	2.5	7	2.5
6	1.5	6	1.5	8	3
3	1	7	3	5	2
3	1	8	2	9	3
	$T_1 = 5.5$		$T_2 = 11$		$T_3 = 13.5$

$\chi_r^2 = 6.7$

Question 21

(a) The hypothesis is that most sentences will be recalled in condition 1 (short sentences) with less good performance in conditions 2 and 3. For Page's L, regardless of the predicted order of word recall, the conditions have to be re-ordered from lowest to highest. This means that condition 3 (long sentences) will be placed on the left because it has the lowest predicted mean.

Table A.6 Page's L trend test (Question 21)

Condition 1 (old 3)	Ranks	Condition 2 (old 2)	Ranks	Condition 3 (old 1)	Ranks
3	1	7	2	8	3
3	1	5	2	10	3
4	2	2	1	9	3
1	1	4	2	7	3
6	2	5	1	11	3
	$T_1 = 7$		$T_2 = 8$		$T_3 = 15$

So the order of conditions should be from predicted lowest scores (i.e. old condition 3) on the left to the predicted highest scores (old condition 1) on the right. The conditions should be reordered (and renumbered) as shown in Table A.6.

(b) Follow the instructions in Box D to calculate $L = 68$. If you got a different answer check that you started by ranking the three scores for each subject *horizontally* across conditions. In Table D the calculated value of $L = 68$ for $C = 3$, $N = 5$, is equal to the required value of 68 at the $p < 0.01$ level. The null hypothesis can be rejected and the results accepted as supporting the predicted trend. Remember that the original hypothesis was that recall scores would be highest in condition 1, lower in condition 2 and worst in condition 3 (long sentences).

Question 22

(a) The means are shown in Table A.7.

(b) Check that you have ranked all the scores as an *overall* set of scores across all conditions before calculating the rank totals as shown in Table A.7. Calculate H following the step-by-step instructions in Box E. In Table E the calculated $H = 6.11$ for group sizes of 4, 4, 4 is larger than the value of 5.69 so the results are significant ($p < 0.05$).

(c) Note that the dependent variable was the number of *wrong* moves, i.e. errors, made when solving the problems. So the higher a subject's scores the worse the performance. If you look at the means in Table A.7, subjects in condition 2 (who were just shown how to do the puzzle) performed worst, i.e. made most errors. Subjects in condition 1 and condition 3 performed at about the same level of errors, indicating that written instructions help whether or not subjects are shown how to do the problem.

(d) The difficulty with a related design is that all subjects would have performed under all three conditions. Once the subjects have been given written instructions in condition 1 or condition 3, they could hardly be expected to 'forget' the instructions when doing condition 2. This is the kind of experiment in which it is sensible to use different groups of subjects.

Table A.7 Kruskal–Wallis test (Question 22)

	Condition 1 (instructions only)		Condition 2 (shown solution/ no instructions)		Condition 3 (instructions and shown solution)	
	Scores (1)	Ranks	Scores (2)	Ranks	Scores (3)	Ranks
	20	3.5	25	7.5	19	1.5
	27	9	33	10	20	3.5
	19	1.5	35	11	25	7.5
	23	6	36	12	22	5
Rank totals	$T_1 = 20$		$T_2 = 40.5$		$T_3 = 17.5$	
Means	22.25		32.25		21.5	

(e) Degrees of freedom (df) equals 4 conditions minus 1: $4 - 1 = 3$.
Look at Table F along the row for $df = 3$. $H = 12.50$ is larger than the value of 11.34 for $p < 0.01$.

Question 23

(a) The means are shown in Table A.8.
(b) The order of conditions should be in the order predicted, from smallest recall scores to largest scores (conditions 3, 2, 1 in Table A.8).
(c) The Jonckheere calculations are shown in brackets. Work out the rationale for these yourself from the step-by-step instructions in Box F.

   $A = 42$
   $B = 48$
   $S = 84 - 48 = 36$

(d) In Table G the value of $S = 36$ for $C = 3$, $n = 4$, is larger than 32 so there is a significant trend ($p < 0.01$) in the predicted order with highest recall scores for very common words.

Table A.8 Jonckheere trend test (Question 23)

	Condition 3 (uncommon words)	Condition 2 (fairly common words)	Condition 1 (very common words)
	2 (7)	7 (4)	14
	4 (6)	8 (4)	15
	4 (6)	3 (4)	10
	2 (7)	2 (4)	13
Means	3	5	13

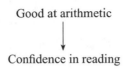

Good at arithmetic

↓

Confidence in reading

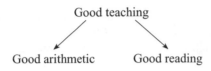

Good at reading

↓

Can read arithmetic problems easily

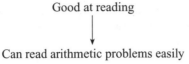

Good teaching

Good arithmetic   Good reading

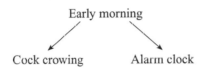

Early morning

Cock crowing   Alarm clock

Figure A.1   Relationship between variables (Question 24)

Question 24

(a) Three possible relationships between reading and arithmetic are shown in Figure A.1.
(b) It is pretty obvious that there is no direct relationship between a cock crowing and an alarm clock going off. They are explained by another variable, 'beginning of the day'.

Question 25

(a) There is usually a high positive correlation between the height of a person and the size of their shoes. This is not a perfect correlation because some tall people have very small feet.
(b) There should be a perfect positive correlation between these variables because the number of tickets sold should exactly correspond to the number of customers (unless, of course, some people manage to slip into the cinema without paying!).
(c) There is most unlikely to be any correlation between the two variables of amount of spinach eaten and the amount of money won on the pools – unfortunately!

Question 26

(a) In winter, the *lower* the temperature, the *higher* electrical bills are likely to be. This is a negative correlation because low temperatures go with high electricity bills. The variables of temperature and the amounts charged for electricity are moving in opposite directions.

(b) There is likely to be a positive correlation between the amount of rain falling and the number of umbrella sales.

Question 27

Children 1, 2 and 3 have high scores on the sports quiz and low scores on the essay. Child 4 has less extreme scores. Child 5 scores almost the same on both, in fact, achieves a higher scores on the quiz than the essay. The scores are still perfectly negatively correlated because relatively higher sports quiz scores go with lower essay scores. Child 5 has the lowest sports quiz score and the highest essay score.

Question 28

(a) The correlations should be listed in the order: 0, 0.5, 0.9.

   (i) 0 is the lowest correlation coefficient because it indicates that there is no correlation at all.
   (ii) 0.5 is next highest because 0.5 is exactly half-way between 0 and 1.
   (iii) 0.9 is the highest positive correlation coefficient because it is only slightly less than a perfect correlation of 1.

(b) There is a high positive correlation between number of miles in a journey and the cost of a railway ticket. But this will *not* be a perfect correlation because on some lines tickets can cost more for slightly shorter journeys. Because of these exceptions, instead of a perfect correlation of 1, there is likely to be a high positive correlation of about 0.9, slightly less than 1.

(c) There is probably a zero correlation between number of pedestrian crossings and average earnings.

Question 29

The negative coefficient of -0.65 represents the highest correlation. This is because it is nearest to $+1$ or -1, both of which indicate a perfect correlation (positive or negative). The positive correlation of $+0.5$ is quite high, but not as high as -0.65. The 0 indicates no correlation at all.

   The number $+1.1$ is a trick because all correlation coefficients have to fall between -1 and $+1$ (see Figure 8.2). Consequently, no correlation coefficient can be higher than 1, so $+1.1$ is an impossible coefficient, being greater than 1.

Question 30

(a) The data in Table 8.2 represent a perfect negative correlation. This is shown in Table A.9, in which the plus and minus differences between the ranked scores are large, giving a correlation coefficient of -1 as a result of the subtraction of 2 from 1 at the end of the calculation.

Table A.9   Spearman negative correlation (Question 30)

Child	Quiz scores	Quiz ranks (A)	Essay scores	Essay ranks (B)	d	d^2
1	10	5	1	1	4	16
2	9	4	2	2	2	4
3	8	3	3	3	0	0
4	7	2	4	4	-2	4
5	6	1	5	5	-4	16
						$\Sigma d^2 = 40$

$$r_S = 1 - \frac{6 \times 40}{5(25 - 1)} = 1 - \frac{240}{5 \times 24} = 1 - \frac{240}{120} = 1 - 2 = -1$$

(b) (i)   The blank columns for the ranks should be filled in as shown in Table A.10. Note that the intermediate answer of 0.46666 etc. is rounded to 0.467, so that the final answer is rounded to 0.533. Note that this is not a very high correlation but it is just high enough to look up its significance in Table H. However, it is not significant even at $p < 0.05$.

Table A.10   Spearman positive correlation (Question 30)

Subject	Shape memory	Ranks A	Spelling	Ranks B	d	d^2
1	7	4	13	3	1	1
2	8	5.5	19	9	-3.5	12.25
3	6	3	16	5.5	-2.5	6.25
4	9	7.5	21	10	-2.5	6.25
5	4	2	10	1	1	1
6	3	1	11	2	-1	1
7	9	7.5	18	7.5	0	0
8	8	5.5	18	7.5	-2	4
9	10	9	14	4	5	25
10	11	10	16	5.5	4.5	20.25
						$\Sigma d^2 = 77$

$$r_S = 1 - \frac{6 \times 77}{10 \times 99} = 1 - 0.467 = 0.533$$

(ii) For 10 subjects, the correlation coefficient values in Table H are 0.564 for $p < 0.05$ and 0.746 for $p < 0.01$. Since the calculated coefficient of 0.533 is smaller than either of these values, this means that the correlation of 0.533 is not significant. There is too high a probability that the results are due to random variability (more than 5 per cent; since the correlation is *not* significant at less than 5 per cent, i.e. $p < 0.05$). So the null hypothesis that there are only random differences between shape memory and spelling ability cannot be rejected.

Question 31

(a) This is an experiment in which the dependent variable would be time scores and the aim would be to look at *differences* in scores between two different groups of subjects in an unrelated design. Looking at Decision Chart 1, the Mann–Whitney would be the appropriate test.
(b) In this experiment subjects would be put into *categories* of solving or not solving the problem. This is all-or-none behaviour, either solving or failing to solve the problem. This is the kind of data which requires the chi-square test.

Question 32

(a) The 15 in cell 2 represents the social science students who reported irregular study patterns. The 23 in cell 3 represents the social science students who reported mixed study patterns.

(b) Technology students reported:

  (i) Regular study patterns: 10
 (ii) Irregular study patterns: 8
(iii) Mixed study patterns: 24

Question 33

(a) Cell 1: 16 and 44
(b) Cell 2: 23 and 44
(c) Cell 3: 47 and 44
(d) Cell 4: 16 and 42
(e) Cell 5: 23 and 42
(f) Cell 6: 47 and 42

Question 34

(a) The independent variable was giving different instructions about helping behaviour. The dependent variable was whether subjects displayed helping behaviour by helping an elderly person across a busy road.

Table A.11 Chi-square test (Question 34)

Marginal
totals

			Marginal totals
Cell 1		Cell 2	
	9	6	15
Cell 3		Cell 4	
	3	12	15
Marginal totals	12	18	(N) 30

Cell 1 $E = \dfrac{12 \times 15}{30} = 6$

Cell 2 $E = \dfrac{18 \times 15}{30} = 9$

Cell 3 $E = \dfrac{12 \times 15}{30} = 6$

Cell 4 $E = \dfrac{18 \times 15}{30} = 9$

$$\chi^2 = \frac{(9-6)^2}{6} + \frac{(6-9)^2}{9} + \frac{(3-6)^2}{6} + \frac{(12-9)^2}{9} = 5$$

$df = (r-1)(c-1) = (2-1) \times (2-1) = 1$

(b) There were 15 subjects in group 1, 9 of whom helped and 6 of whom did not help. The were 15 subjects in group 2, 3 of whom helped and 12 of whom did not help.

(c) Using the marginal totals in Table A.11, calculate the expected frequencies. Refer back to the step-by-step instructions in Box H. Remember that the observed frequencies are shown in Table A.11 and the expected frequencies are calculated by multiplying the two relevant marginal totals and dividing by N.

(d) The experimental hypothesis was one-tailed because the prediction was that subjects in group 1 would be more likely to help than group 2. χ^2 can only indicate whether there are overall differences between the cells but in a 2×2 table it is easier to relate the categories to the original hypothesis. With $df = 1$, the calculated χ^2 of 5 is larger than 3.84, so the differences between the cells are significant ($p < 0.05$).

Question 35

(a) Passing or failing an exam can only be measured on a nominal scale, each grade being allocated into one of two categories of either pass or fail.

(b) Teachers' ratings would be ordinal because they would imply a certain order from best to worse, but it would not be certain that there are equal intervals between the teachers' grades.

(c) Scores on a test are usually treated as *interval* data. However, treating them as interval data makes the assumption that the scores do represent *equal* intervals along a continuous numerical scale of arithmetical ability.

Question 36

The answers are 100 and 9.

Question 37

(a) Σx^2 is the sum of the squares of each individual score: $16 + 25 + 49 + 64 + 100 = 254$.

(b) $(\Sigma x)^2$ is the total of the scores $(4 + 5 + 7 + 8 + 10)$ squared: $34^2 = 1156$.

Question 38

(a) The total score for condition 4 equals the total for all subjects minus the totals for conditions 1, 2, 3. The condition 4 total score is therefore:

$$56 - (8 + 12 + 20) = 56 - 40 = 16$$

(b) There are $4 - 1 = 3$ degrees of freedom for conditions. This is because it is possible to calculate the total for one condition from the other three so one of the conditions is not 'free to vary'.

(c) The total number of subjects (N) is 16. It would be possible to calculate one subject's scores from the other 15. So $N - 1$ represents the degrees of freedom, $16 - 1 = 15$.

Question 39

Between (4) *conditions variance* df_{bet} $C - 1 = 3$
$N = 4$ subjects × 4 conditions   16
Total variance df_{total} $N - 1 = 15$
Error variance df_{error} $(N - 1) - (C - 1) = 15 - 3 = 12$

Note that the degrees of freedom for *between variance* (3) and *error variance* (12) always add up to the *total variance df* (15).

Question 40

(a) The means are shown in Table A.12.

(b) See Table A.12 for the calculation of $t = 3.15$. Remember that when calculating Σd both pluses and minuses are taken into account.

Table A.12 t test related (Question 40)

Subjects	Condition 1	Condition 2	d	d^2
1	6	2	4	16
2	7	1	6	36
3	8	3	5	25
4	10	4	6	36
5	8	3	5	25
6	8	2	6	36
7	5	7	−2	4
8	3	4	−1	1
Means	6.88	3.25	$\Sigma d = 29$	$\Sigma d^2 = 179$

$$(\Sigma d)^2 = 29 \times 29 = 841$$

$$t = \frac{29}{\sqrt{\dfrac{8 \times 179 - 841}{7}}}$$

$$= \frac{29}{\sqrt{84.43}}$$

$$= \frac{29}{9.189}$$

$$= 3.15$$

(c) $df = N - 1 = 8 - 1 = 7$

Along the $df = 7$ row in Table I, the calculated $t = 3.15$ is larger than 2.998. It can be concluded that the results of the experiment are supported, $p < 0.01$ (one-tailed).

Question 41

(a) The experiment compared subjects' recall scores for simple and complex tests. On balance it might be better to use the same subjects. The texts are different (simple or complex) and the order of presentation can be counterbalanced. Using the same subjects means that individual differences in learning are the same for the two conditions.

   With different subjects the better learners might have been allocated to the simple texts, thus inflating the scores for that condition. On the other hand, using different groups, the researcher could be sure that learning one text could not have any influence on learning the other.

   Look back to Chapter 2, Sections 2.3 and 2.4 and Progress box two, to refresh your understanding of the advantages and disadvantages of using same subjects (related) or different subjects (unrelated).

(b) Both the unrelated t and Mann–Whitney are suitable for analysing differences between two conditions for unrelated designs using different subjects. The distinction between the tests is that the Mann–Whitney uses the 'cruder' method of ranking scores. The t test can calculate precise variances. On the other hand, as a parametric test, it has to meet the requirements for parametric tests (see Chapter 10).

Question 42

(a) Working through Box K, we obtain the following:

$$SS_{bet} = \frac{\Sigma T^2}{n} - \frac{(\Sigma x)^2}{N} = \frac{30^2 + 17^2}{5} - \frac{47^2}{10} \qquad df = 1$$

$$= 237.8 - 220.9 = 16.9$$

$$SS_{tot} = \Sigma x^2 - \frac{(\Sigma x)^2}{N} = 269 - 220.9 = 48.1 \qquad df = 9$$

$$SS_{error} = SS_{tot} - SS_{bet} = 48.1 - 16.9 = 31.2 \qquad df = 8$$

$$MS_{bet} = \frac{SS_{bet}}{df_{bet}} = \frac{16.9}{1} = 16.9$$

$$MS_{error} = \frac{SS_{error}}{df_{error}} = \frac{31.2}{8} = 3.9$$

$$F_{1,8} = \frac{MS_{bet}}{MS_{error}} = \frac{16.9}{3.9} = 4.33$$

The ANOVA table is as shown in Table A.13.

(b) The calculated value of $F_{1,8} = 4.33$ is smaller than the value of 5.32 in Table J(1) for $v_1 = 1$ and $v_2 = 8$. The results are not significant even at the $p < 0.05$ so the null hypothesis that the results are due to random error cannot be rejected.

(c) The one-way unrelated ANOVA is normally used for three conditions. However, you have seen that it can also be used where there are only two conditions. When there are only two conditions we can also use the t test (unrelated); see Chapter 12, Section 12.2. The methods for analysing the data in Table 13.5 using ANOVA or the t test are actually quite similar. However, the t test is usually used for analysing two conditions because the probabilities in Table I have been specifically calculated for this purpose.

Table A.13   One-way unrelated ANOVA (Question 42)

Sources of variance	SS	df	MS	F ratio
Between conditions	16.9	1	16.9	$F_{1,8} = 4.33$
Error	31.2	8	3.9	
Total	48.1	9		

Question 43

(a) $SS_{bet} = \dfrac{27^2 + 16^2}{5} - \dfrac{43^2}{10} = 197 - 184.9 = 12.1 \qquad df = 1$

$SS_{subj} = \dfrac{5^2 + 10^2 + 7^2 + 12^2 + 9^2}{2} - 184.9$

$= 199.5 - 184.9 = 14.6 \qquad\qquad df = 4$

$SS_{tot} = 221 - 184.9 = 36.1 \qquad\qquad df = 9$

$SS_{error} = 36.1 - 12.1 - 14.6 = 9.4 \qquad df = 4$

$MS_{bet} = 12.1$

$MS_{subj} = 3.65$

$MS_{error} = 2.35$

(b) The $F_{1,4}$ statistic for between conditions is calculated by dividing MS_{bet} by MS_{error} giving 5.149. The $F_{4,4}$ for subjects is 1.55. Looking up these values of F in Table J(1) shows that neither the between-conditions variance nor the subjects variance is significant. Note that again there are only two conditions that could have been analysed using the t test (related).

Question 44

Cell 1 (less good readers with no reading scheme) is condition 1.
Cell 2 (good readers with no reading scheme) is condition 2.
Cell 3 (less good readers with reading scheme) is condition 3.
Cell 4 (good readers with reading scheme) is condition 4.

Question 45

The total score of 16 for good readers gives the overall score for good readers regardless of whether they are exposed to a reading scheme or not.

The total score of 9 for less good readers gives the overall score for less good readers whether they are exposed to a reading scheme or not.

This difference between the overall scores of 9 for less good readers and 16 for good readers represents the main effect of being good or less good at reading. It is a main effect because it compares the overall effect of variable B (reading skills) taking no account of variable A (reading scheme).

Question 46

(a) The experimental hypothesis would predict that condition 2 and condition 3 would produce better recall of texts because these are the conditions in which the title is compatible with the text.

(b) (i) The overall scores for variable B (texts about furniture and animals) both total 25, as shown in the totals at the right-hand side.

(ii) The overall scores for variable A (furniture and animals titles) also happen both to add up to 25 each, as shown by the totals at the bottom of the table.

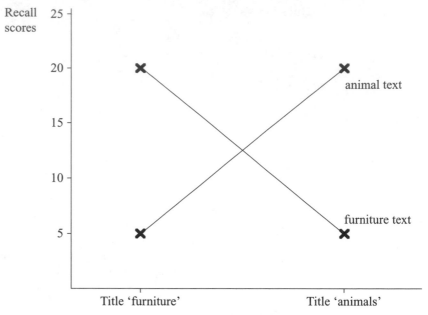

Figure A.2   Graph showing interaction (Question 46)

    (iii) Because there are no overall differences between the two texts (25 each) nor for the two titles (25 each), there are no main effects for variable *A* or variable *B* on their own. This is not surprising because the hypothesis predicted an interaction between the two variables depending on whether text and title are compatible. In fact, it would be quite awkward for the experimenter if one of the texts had been easier to learn regardless of the title.

(c) The graph demonstrating the interaction between the variables is shown in Figure A.2. There is a complete interaction between the text and titles because, as predicted, the slopes actually cross over. The recall scores for the furniture text is influenced by whether the title is 'furniture' or 'animals' and the same goes for the animals text. The fact that one variable influences the other indicates that there is an interaction between the two independent variables.

Question 47

(a) The means for the four conditions in Table 15.3 are:

Condition 1	Condition 2	Condition 3	Condition 4
3	5	8	11

(b) In Table 15.4 the three scores for textbook *X* studied for a short period (condition 1) have been put in cell 1; the three scores for Textbook *X* studied for a long period (condition 2) have been put in cell 3; the three scores for textbook *Y* studied for a short period (condition 3) have been put in cell 2; the three scores for textbook *Y* studied for a long period (condition 4) have been put in cell 4.

Question 48

The total of all the individual scores	=	85
(9, 8, 6, 7, 5, 3, 3, 4, etc.)		
The cell totals (30, 15, 15, 25)	=	85
The side totals (45, 40)	=	85
The bottom totals (45, 40)	=	85

Question 49

(a) The filled-in ANOVA sources of variance table is shown in Table A.14.
(b) The sums of squares, mean squares and F ratios are shown in Table A.14.
(c) Yes. Variable A and the interaction of variables $A \times B$ have a significant effect on the scores. The F ratio of 15.06 for variable A for $v_1 = 1$ and $v_2 = 12$ is significant in Table J(3) at the $p < 0.01$ level (larger than the value of $F_{1,12} = 9.33$) and the interaction between the two variables of 33.96 is significant for $F_{2,12}$ in Table J(4) at the $p < 0.001$ level.

Table A.14 ANOVA 2×3 table (Question 49)

Source of variance	SS	df	MS	F ratios
Variable A	14.22	1	14.22	$F_{1,12} = 15.06$
Variable B	4.33	2	2.165	$F_{2,12} = 2.29$
$A \times B$ (interaction)	64.12	2	32.06	$F_{2,12} = 33.96$
Error	11.33	12	0.944	
Total	94.00	17		

Question 50

(a) Not surprisingly Figure A.3, which uses the same scores in a different orientation, shows the same relationships between variables as in Figure 15.2.
(b) More short words are recalled than long words and slow rates of presentation produce better recall overall. There is no interaction between the two variables.
(c) These results contradict those found in the unrelated ANOVA experiment described in Section 15.2. In that experiment the means, the ANOVA analysis and the graph in Figure 15.1 showed a significant interaction between length of word and rate of presentation. There were no overall differences between long or short words or length of presentation time. All this goes to show is that small changes, perhaps in the words which were presented or the selected presentation times, can produce conflicting results.

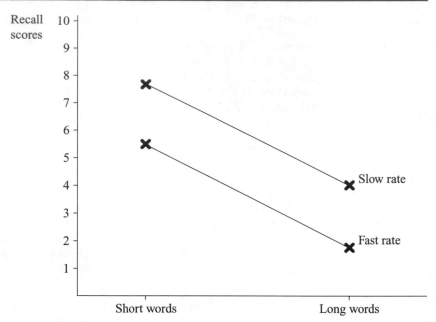

Figure A.3   Graph for related ANOVA (Question 50)

Question 51

If you look at Decision Chart 1 inside the front cover, you will see that the appropriate related trend test for same subjects is Page's *L* trend test.

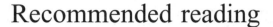

Recommended reading

There are a few books which provide some useful insights into experimental design and statistics.

One general book is *Research Methods and Statistics in Psychology* by Hugh Coolican. This book gives an introduction to designing experiments and other types of research. Ethics are taken into consideration and there are useful hints about describing data and writing up research reports. The statistics are quite simple, but there are other compensations. Another book which covers much of the same ground is *Designing and Reporting Experiments* by Peter Harris.

Siegel's book, *Nonparametric Statistics for the Behavioural Sciences*, is a classic book on non-parametric tests. In fact, it was Siegel who made these tests so popular. He gives techniques like the Fisher–Yates test which can deal with small numbers for the chi-square mentioned in Chapter 9.

There are also more advanced statistic textbooks. These tend to assume quite a lot of knowledge and tend to be couched in mathematical language. They contain calculations for the Tukey test for looking at comparisons between ANOVA conditions which was described in Chapter 15, Section 15.5. Two recent books are *Doing Quantitative Psychological Research* by David Clark-Carter and *Data Analysis for Psychology* by George Dunbar.

Finally, there are many manuals for computerized statistical packages. One of the most commonly used programs is SPSS which can be used on either PC or Macintosh. These are two useful books published by Psychology Press, one on *SPSS for Windows Made Simple* (for PCs) and the other on *SPSS for Macintosh Made Simple*.

References

Clark-Carter, D. (1997) *Doing Quantitative Psychological Research: From Design to Report*. Hove: Psychology Press.

Coolican, H. (1999) *Research Methods and Statistics in Psychology* (3rd edition). London: Hodder & Stoughton.

Dunbar, G. (1998) *Data Analysis for Psychology*. London: Arnold.

Gray, C.D. and Kinnear, P.R. (1998) *SPSS for Macintosh Made Simple*. Hove: Psychology Press.

Harris, P. (1986) *Designing and Reporting Experiments*. Milton Keynes: Open University Press.

Kinnear, P.R. and Gray, C.D. (1999) *SPSS for Windows Made Simple* (3rd edition). Hove: Psychology Press.

Siegel, S. (1956) *Nonparametric Statistics for the Behavioural Sciences*. New York: McGraw-Hill.

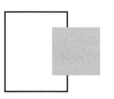

Appendix 1:
Computer statistical packages

These were first introduced in Chapter 14, Section 14.7. It would probably be a good idea to turn back to that section and read the 'health warnings' about the indiscriminate use of statistics packages. However, these computerized packages certainly take the sweat out of doing calculations by hand – as long as you do not lose sight of the aims and analysis of psychological research.

Most statistical packages have many different types of statistics, including non-parametric tests. However, these are so easy to do by hand that we will be concentrating on parametric tests like the t tests and ANOVA.

A *sixth word of advice* to be added to the five given in Section 14.7 is not to get carried away by all the options available in computer packages. It is fatal to undertake additional analysis of the data if you do not understand the purpose of the analysis. You can use any type of multivariable ANOVA described in this book, including mixed ANOVA. We introduced the notion of the Tukey Test so that you will be able to understand computer packages which include individual comparisons to sort out the overall significance of ANOVA (see Chapter 15, Section 15.5).

A matter of terminology

In order to use a particular package you will have to study a manual which gives precise logging-in instructions. In this book we have used the terminology of independent and dependent variables. On each variable there may be a number of conditions. In 2×2 ANOVA there are two or more conditions on each variable. This terminology is perfectly acceptable and we have been consistent in referring to variables (because they vary) and experimental conditions.

However, some statistical packages use different terminology. They all refer to the same concepts, so it is just a matter of learning the appropriate terminology for each computer package.

SPSS terminology

SPSS for Windows is perhaps the most commonly used statistical program. It has been designed to run on both PCs and Macs (see references in the Reading List).

In general the use of variable is consistent with ours. But some packages use the word 'factors' for variables. So you will often be instructed to indicate how many *factors* you are using. For instance, if you are investigating two independent variables in a two-way ANOVA, the instructions may ask you to identify two factors, e.g. word length and presentation rate.

Another usage that could be puzzling is that, rather than related or unrelated designs, the terminology refers to *between groups* and *within groups*. You will remember that in Chapter 2, Sections 2.3 and 2.4, we introduced both terms, *between-subjects* or *unrelated designs* and *within-subjects* or *related designs*, as listed in Progress box two.

When the same subjects are being used in a within-subjects or related design, the idea is that all comparisons are 'within' the same groups of subjects whose scores are related. When different subjects are being used, all comparisons are between different groups of subjects whose scores are unrelated.

▶ **Progress box fourteen**

Terminology

Independent variables	Factors
Conditions on each variable	Levels of factors
One-way ANOVA	One factor
Two-way ANOVA	Multifactorial
Within-subjects/related	Within-groups factor
Between-subjects/unrelated	Between groups factor

Appendix 2:
Statistical tables

Table A   Critical values of W at various levels of probability (Wilcoxon)

The statistic W denotes the smaller sum of total signed ranks. For any N (number of subjects minus ties) the observed value of W is significant at a given level of significance if it is *equal to* or *less than* the critical values shown in the table.

	Level of significance for one-tailed test					Level of significance for one-tailed test			
	0.05	0.025	0.01	0.005		0.05	0.025	0.01	0.005
	Level of significance for two-tailed test					Level of significance for two-tailed test			
N	0.10	0.05	0.02	0.01	N	0.10	0.05	0.02	0.01
5	1	–	–	–	28	130	117	102	92
6	2	1	–	–	29	141	127	111	100
7	4	2	0	–	30	152	137	120	109
8	6	4	2	0	31	163	148	130	118
9	8	6	3	2	32	175	159	141	128
10	11	8	5	3	33	188	171	151	138
11	14	11	7	5	34	201	183	162	149
12	17	14	10	7	35	214	195	174	160
13	21	17	13	10	36	228	208	186	171
14	26	21	16	13	37	242	222	198	183
15	30	25	20	16	38	256	235	211	195
16	36	30	24	19	39	271	250	224	208
17	41	35	28	23	40	287	264	238	221
18	47	40	33	28	41	303	279	252	234
19	54	46	38	32	42	319	295	267	248
20	60	52	43	37	43	336	311	281	262
21	68	59	49	43	44	353	327	297	277
22	75	66	56	49	45	371	344	313	292
23	83	73	62	55	46	389	361	329	307
24	92	81	69	61	47	408	379	345	323
25	101	90	77	68	48	427	397	362	339
26	110	98	85	76	49	446	415	380	356
27	120	107	93	84	50	466	434	398	373

*Dashes in the body of the table indicate that no decision is possible at the stated level of significance because the numbers of subjects are too small.

Table B Critical values of U at various levels of probability (Mann–Whitney)

For any n_1 and n_2 the observed value of U is significant at a given level of significance if it is *equal to* or *less than* the critical values shown in the Tables B(1)–B(4).

Table B(1) Critical values of U for a one-tailed test at 0.005; two-tailed test at 0.01*

										n_1										
n_2	1	2	3	4	5	6	7	8	9	10	11	12	13	14	15	16	17	18	19	20
1	–	–	–	–	–	–	–	–	–	–	–	–	–	–	–	–	–	–	–	–
2	–	–	–	–	–	–	–	–	–	–	–	–	–	–	–	–	–	–	0	0
3	–	–	–	–	–	–	–	–	0	0	0	1	1	1	2	2	2	2	3	3
4	–	–	–	–	–	0	0	1	1	2	2	3	3	4	5	5	6	6	7	8
5	–	–	–	–	0	1	1	2	3	4	5	6	7	7	8	9	10	11	12	13
6	–	–	–	0	1	2	3	4	5	6	7	9	10	11	12	13	15	16	17	18
7	–	–	–	0	1	3	4	6	7	9	10	12	13	15	16	18	19	21	22	24
8	–	–	–	1	2	4	6	7	9	11	13	15	17	18	20	22	24	26	28	30
9	–	–	0	1	3	5	7	9	11	13	16	18	20	22	24	27	29	31	33	36
10	–	–	0	2	4	6	9	11	13	16	18	21	24	26	29	31	34	37	39	42
11	–	–	0	2	5	7	10	13	16	18	21	24	27	30	33	36	39	42	45	48
12	–	–	1	3	6	9	12	15	18	21	24	27	31	34	37	41	44	47	51	54
13	–	–	1	3	7	10	13	17	20	24	27	31	34	38	42	45	49	53	56	60
14	–	–	1	4	7	11	15	18	22	26	30	34	38	42	46	50	54	58	63	67
15	–	–	2	5	8	12	16	20	24	29	33	37	42	46	51	55	60	64	69	73
16	–	–	2	5	9	13	18	22	27	31	36	41	45	50	55	60	65	70	74	79
17	–	–	2	6	10	15	19	24	29	34	39	44	49	54	60	65	70	75	81	86
18	–	–	2	6	11	16	21	26	31	37	42	47	53	58	64	70	75	81	87	92
19	–	0	3	7	12	17	22	28	33	39	45	51	56	63	69	74	81	87	93	99
20	–	0	3	8	13	18	24	30	36	42	48	54	60	67	73	79	86	92	99	105

*Dashes in the body of the table indicate that no decision is possible at the stated level of significance because the numbers of subjects are too small.

Table B(2)   Critical values of U for a one-tailed test at 0.01; two-tailed test at 0.02*

n_2	n_1																			
	1	*2*	*3*	*4*	*5*	*6*	*7*	*8*	*9*	*10*	*11*	*12*	*13*	*14*	*15*	*16*	*17*	*18*	*19*	*20*
1	–	–	–	–	–	–	–	–	–	–	–	–	–	–	–	–	–	–	–	–
2	–	–	–	–	–	–	–	–	–	–	–	–	0	0	0	0	0	0	1	1
3	–	–	–	–	–	–	0	0	1	1	1	2	2	2	3	3	4	4	4	5
4	–	–	–	–	0	1	1	2	3	3	4	5	5	6	7	7	8	9	9	10
5	–	–	–	0	1	2	3	4	5	6	7	8	9	10	11	12	13	14	15	16
6	–	–	–	1	2	3	4	6	7	8	9	11	12	13	15	16	18	19	20	22
7	–	–	0	1	3	4	6	7	9	11	12	14	16	17	19	21	23	24	26	28
8	–	–	0	2	4	6	7	9	11	13	15	17	20	22	24	26	28	30	32	34
9	–	–	1	3	5	7	9	11	14	16	18	21	23	26	28	31	33	36	38	40
10	–	–	1	3	6	8	11	13	16	19	22	24	27	30	33	36	38	41	44	47
11	–	–	1	4	7	9	12	15	18	22	25	28	31	34	37	41	44	47	50	53
12	–	–	2	5	8	11	14	17	21	24	28	31	35	38	42	46	49	53	56	60
13	–	0	2	5	9	12	16	20	23	27	31	35	39	43	47	51	55	59	63	67
14	–	0	2	6	10	13	17	22	26	30	34	38	43	47	51	56	60	65	69	73
15	–	0	3	7	11	15	19	24	28	33	37	42	47	51	56	61	66	70	75	80
16	–	0	3	7	12	16	21	26	31	36	41	46	51	56	61	66	71	76	82	87
17	–	0	4	8	13	18	23	28	33	38	44	49	55	60	66	71	77	82	88	93
18	–	0	4	9	14	19	24	30	36	41	47	53	59	65	70	76	82	88	94	100
19	–	1	4	9	15	20	26	32	38	44	50	56	63	69	75	82	88	94	101	107
20	–	1	5	10	16	22	28	34	40	47	53	60	67	73	80	87	93	100	107	114

*Dashes in the body of the table indicate that no decision is possible at the stated level of significance because the numbers of subjects are too small.

Appendix 2: Statistical tables

Table B(3) Critical values of U for a one-tailed test at 0.025; two-tailed test at 0.05*

										n_1										
n_2	*1*	*2*	*3*	*4*	*5*	*6*	*7*	*8*	*9*	*10*	*11*	*12*	*13*	*14*	*15*	*16*	*17*	*18*	*19*	*20*
1	–	–	–	–	–	–	–	–	–	–	–	–	–	–	–	–	–	–	–	–
2	–	–	–	–	–	–	–	0	0	0	0	1	1	1	1	1	2	2	2	2
3	–	–	–	–	0	1	1	2	2	3	3	4	4	5	5	6	6	7	7	8
4	–	–	–	0	1	2	3	4	4	5	6	7	8	9	10	11	11	12	13	13
5	–	–	0	1	2	3	5	6	7	8	9	11	12	13	14	15	17	18	19	20
6	–	–	1	2	3	5	6	8	10	11	13	14	16	17	19	21	22	24	25	27
7	–	–	1	3	5	6	8	10	12	14	16	18	20	22	24	26	28	30	32	34
8	–	0	2	4	6	8	10	13	15	17	19	22	24	26	29	31	34	36	38	41
9	–	0	2	4	7	10	12	15	17	20	23	26	28	31	34	37	39	42	45	48
10	–	0	3	5	8	11	14	17	20	23	26	29	33	36	39	42	45	48	52	55
11	–	0	3	6	9	13	16	19	23	26	30	33	37	40	44	47	51	55	58	62
12	–	1	4	7	11	14	18	22	26	29	33	37	41	45	49	53	57	61	65	69
13	–	1	4	8	12	16	20	24	28	33	37	41	45	50	54	59	63	67	72	76
14	–	1	5	9	13	17	22	26	31	36	40	45	50	55	59	64	67	74	78	83
15	–	1	5	10	14	19	24	29	34	39	44	49	54	59	64	70	75	80	85	90
16	–	1	6	11	15	21	26	31	37	42	47	53	59	64	70	75	81	86	92	98
17	–	2	6	11	17	22	28	34	39	45	51	57	63	67	75	81	87	93	99	105
18	–	2	7	12	18	24	30	36	42	48	55	61	67	74	80	86	93	99	106	112
19	–	2	7	13	19	25	32	38	45	52	58	65	72	78	85	92	99	106	113	119
20	–	2	8	13	20	27	34	41	48	55	62	69	76	83	90	98	105	112	119	127

*Dashes in the body of the table indicate that no decision is possible at the stated level of significance because the numbers of subjects are too small.

Table B(4) Critical values of U for a one-tailed test at 0.05; two-tailed test at 0.10*

	n_1																			
n_2	1	2	3	4	5	6	7	8	9	10	11	12	13	14	15	16	17	18	19	20
1	–	–	–	–	–	–	–	–	–	–	–	–	–	–	–	–	–	–	0	0
2	–	–	–	–	0	0	0	1	1	1	1	2	2	2	3	3	3	4	4	4
3	–	–	0	0	1	2	2	3	3	4	5	5	6	7	7	8	9	9	10	11
4	–	–	0	1	2	3	4	5	6	7	8	9	10	11	12	14	15	16	17	18
5	–	0	1	2	4	5	6	8	9	11	12	13	15	16	18	19	20	22	23	25
6	–	0	2	3	5	7	8	10	12	14	16	17	19	21	23	25	26	28	30	32
7	–	0	2	4	6	8	11	13	15	17	19	21	24	26	28	30	33	35	37	39
8	–	1	3	5	8	10	13	15	18	20	23	26	28	31	33	36	39	41	44	47
9	–	1	3	6	9	12	15	18	21	24	27	30	33	36	39	42	45	48	51	54
10	–	1	4	7	11	14	17	20	24	27	31	34	37	41	44	48	51	55	58	62
11	–	1	5	8	12	16	19	23	27	31	34	38	42	46	50	54	57	61	65	69
12	–	2	5	9	13	17	21	26	30	34	38	42	47	51	55	60	64	68	72	77
13	–	2	6	10	15	19	24	28	33	37	42	47	51	56	61	65	70	75	80	84
14	–	2	7	11	16	21	26	31	36	41	46	51	56	61	66	71	77	82	87	92
15	–	3	7	12	18	23	28	33	39	44	50	55	61	66	72	77	83	88	94	100
16	–	3	8	14	19	25	30	36	42	48	54	60	65	71	77	83	89	95	101	107
17	–	3	9	15	20	26	33	39	45	51	57	64	70	77	83	89	96	102	109	115
18	–	4	9	16	22	28	35	41	48	55	61	68	75	82	88	95	102	109	116	123
19	0	4	10	17	23	30	37	44	51	58	65	72	80	87	94	101	109	116	123	130
20	0	4	11	18	25	32	39	47	54	62	69	77	84	92	100	107	115	123	130	138

*Dashes in the body of the table indicate that no decision is possible at the stated level of significance because the numbers of subjects are too small.

Table C   Critical values of χ_r^2 at various levels of probability (Friedman)

For any C and N the observed value of χ_r^2 is significant at a given level of significance if it is *equal to* or *larger than* the critical values shown in Tables C(1) and C(2).

Table C(1) Critical values for three conditions ($C = 3$)

$N = 2$		$N = 3$		$N = 4$		$N = 5$	
χ_r^2	p	χ_r^2	p	χ_r^2	p	χ_r^2	p
0	1.000	0.000	1.000	0.0	1.000	0.0	1.000
1	0.833	0.667	0.944	0.5	0.931	0.4	0.954
3	0.500	2.000	0.528	1.5	0.653	1.2	0.691
4	0.167	2.667	0.361	2.0	0.431	1.6	0.522
		4.667	0.194	3.5	0.273	2.8	0.367
		6.000	0.028	4.5	0.125	3.6	0.182
				6.0	0.069	4.8	0.124
				6.5	0.042	5.2	0.093
				8.0	0.0046	6.4	0.039
						7.6	0.024
						8.4	0.0085
						10.0	0.00077

$N = 6$		$N = 7$		$N = 8$		$N = 9$	
χ_r^2	p	χ_r^2	p	χ_r^2	p	χ_r^2	p
0.00	1.000	0.000	1.000	0.00	1.000	0.000	1.000
0.33	0.956	0.286	0.964	0.25	0.967	0.222	0.971
1.00	0.740	0.857	0.768	0.75	0.794	0.667	0.814
1.33	0.570	1.143	0.620	1.00	0.654	0.889	0.865
2.33	0.430	2.000	0.486	1.75	0.531	1.556	0.569
3.00	0.252	2.571	0.305	2.25	0.355	2.000	0.398
4.00	0.184	3.429	0.237	3.00	0.285	2.667	0.328
4.33	0.142	3.714	0.192	3.25	0.236	2.889	0.278
5.33	0.072	4.571	0.112	4.00	0.149	3.556	0.187
6.33	0.052	5.429	0.085	4.75	0.120	4.222	0.154
7.00	0.029	6.000	0.052	5.25	0.079	4.667	0.107
8.33	0.012	7.143	0.027	6.25	0.047	5.556	0.069
9.00	0.0081	7.714	0.021	6.75	0.038	6.000	0.057
9.33	0.0055	8.000	0.016	7.00	0.030	6.222	0.048
10.33	0.0017	8.857	0.0084	7.75	0.018	6.889	0.031
12.00	0.00013	10.286	0.0036	9.00	0.0099	8.000	0.019
		10.571	0.0027	9.25	0.0080	8.222	0.016
		11.143	0.0012	9.75	0.0048	8.667	0.010
		12.286	0.00032	10.75	0.0024	9.556	0.0060
		14.000	0.000021	12.00	0.0011	10.667	0.0035
				12.25	0.00086	10.889	0.0029
				13.00	0.00026	11.556	0.0013
				14.25	0.000061	12.667	0.00066
				16.00	0.0000036	13.556	0.00035
						14.000	0.00020
						14.222	0.000097
						14.889	0.000054
						16.222	0.000011
						18.000	0.0000006

Table C(2)   Critical values for four conditions ($C = 4$)

χ_r^2	p	χ_r^2	p	χ_r^2	p	χ_r^2	p
N = 2		N = 3		N = 4			
0.0	1.000	0.0	1.000	0.0	1.000	5.7	0.141
0.6	0.958	0.6	0.958	0.3	0.992	6.0	0.105
1.2	0.834	1.0	0.910	0.6	0.928	6.3	0.094
1.8	0.792	1.8	0.727	0.9	0.900	6.6	0.077
2.4	0.625	2.2	0.608	1.2	0.800	6.9	0.068
3.0	0.542	2.6	0.524	1.5	0.754	7.2	0.054
3.6	0.458	3.4	0.446	1.8	0.677	7.5	0.052
4.2	0.375	3.8	0.342	2.1	0.649	7.8	0.036
4.8	0.208	4.2	0.300	2.4	0.524	8.1	0.033
5.4	0.167	5.0	0.207	2.7	0.508	8.4	0.019
6.0	0.042	5.4	0.175	3.0	0.432	8.7	0.014
		5.8	0.148	3.3	0.389	9.3	0.012
		6.6	0.075	3.6	0.355	9.6	0.0069
		7.0	0.054	3.9	0.324	9.9	0.0062
		7.4	0.033	4.5	0.242	10.2	0.0027
		8.2	0.017	4.8	0.200	10.8	0.0016
		9.0	0.0017	5.1	0.190	11.1	0.00094
				5.4	0.158	12.0	0.000072

Table D   Critical values of Page's L (one-tailed) at various levels of probability

For any N (number of subjects) and C the observed value of L is significant at a given level of significance if it is *equal to* or *larger than* the critical values shown in the table.

| N | C (number of conditions) | | | | p < |
	3	4	5	6	
2	–	–	109	178	0.001
	–	60	106	173	0.01
	28	58	103	166	0.05
3	–	89	160	260	0.001
	42	87	155	252	0.01
	41	84	150	244	0.05
4	56	117	210	341	0.001
	55	114	204	331	0.01
	54	111	197	321	0.05
5	70	145	259	420	0.001
	68	141	251	409	0.01
	66	137	244	397	0.05
6	83	172	307	499	0.001
	81	167	299	486	0.01
	79	163	291	474	0.05
7	96	198	355	577	0.001
	93	193	346	563	0.01
	91	189	338	550	0.05
8	109	225	403	655	0.001
	106	220	393	640	0.01
	104	214	384	625	0.05
9	121	252	451	733	0.001
	119	246	441	717	0.01
	116	240	431	701	0.05
10	134	278	499	811	0.001
	131	272	487	793	0.01
	128	266	477	777	0.05
11	147	305	546	888	0.001
	144	298	534	869	0.01
	141	292	523	852	0.05
12	160	331	593	965	0.001
	156	324	581	946	0.01
	153	317	570	928	0.05

Table E Critical values of H at various levels of probability (Kruskal–Wallis)

For any n_1, n_2, n_3 the observed value of H is significant at a given level of significance if it is *equal to* or *larger than* the critical values shown in the table.

Size of groups					Size of groups				
n_1	n_2	n_3	H	p	n_1	n_2	n_3	H	p
2	1	1	2.7000	0.500	4	3	1	5.8333	0.021
2	2	1	3.6000	0.200				5.2083	0.050
2	2	2	4.5714	0.067				5.0000	0.057
			3.7143	0.200				4.0556	0.093
								3.8889	0.129
3	1	1	3.2000	0.300	4	3	2	6.4444	0.008
3	2	1	4.2857	0.100				6.3000	0.011
			3.8571	0.133				5.4444	0.046
3	2	2	5.3572	0.029				5.4000	0.051
			4.7143	0.048				4.5111	0.098
			4.5000	0.067				4.4444	0.102
			4.4643	0.105	4	3	3	6.7455	0.010
3	3	1	5.1429	0.043				6.7091	0.013
			4.5714	0.100				5.7909	0.046
			4.0000	0.129				5.7273	0.050
3	3	2	6.2500	0.011				4.7091	0.092
			5.3611	0.032				4.7000	0.101
			5.1389	0.061	4	4	1	6.6667	0.010
			4.5556	0.100				6.1667	0.022
			4.2500	0.121				4.9667	0.048
3	3	3	7.2000	0.004				4.8667	0.054
			6.4889	0.011				4.1667	0.082
			5.6889	0.029				4.0667	0.102
			5.6000	0.050	4	4	2	7.0364	0.006
			5.0667	0.086				6.8727	0.011
			4.6222	0.100				5.4545	0.046
4	1	1	3.5714	0.200				5.2364	0.052
4	2	1	4.8214	0.057				4.5545	0.098
			4.5000	0.076				4.4455	0.103
			4.0179	0.114	4	4	3	7.1439	0.010
4	2	2	6.0000	0.014				7.1364	0.011
			5.3333	0.033				5.5985	0.049
			5.1250	0.052				5.5758	0.051
			4.4583	0.100				4.5455	0.099
			4.1667	0.105				4.4773	0.102
					4	4	4	7.6538	0.008
								7.5385	0.011
								5.6923	0.049
								5.6538	0.054
								4.6539	0.097
								4.5001	0.104

Table E *(cont'd)*

Size of groups					Size of groups				
n_1	n_2	n_3	H	p	n_1	n_2	n_3	H	p
5	1	1	3.8571	0.143	5	4	3	7.4449	0.010
								7.3949	0.011
5	2	1	5.2500	0.036				5.6564	0.049
			5.0000	0.048				5.6308	0.050
			4.4500	0.071				4.5487	0.099
			4.2000	0.095				4.5231	0.103
			4.0500	0.119					
					5	4	4	7.7604	0.009
5	2	2	6.5333	0.008				7.7440	0.011
			6.1333	0.013				5.6571	0.049
			5.1600	0.034				5.6176	0.050
			5.0400	0.056				4.6187	0.100
			4.3733	0.090				4.5527	0.102
			4.2933	0.122					
					5	5	1	7.3091	0.009
5	3	1	6.4000	0.012				6.8364	0.011
			4.9600	0.048				5.1273	0.046
			4.8711	0.052				4.9091	0.053
			4.0178	0.095				4.1091	0.086
			3.8400	0.123				4.0364	0.105
5	3	2	6.9091	0.009	5	5	2	7.3385	0.010
			6.8218	0.010				7.2692	0.010
			5.2509	0.049				5.3385	0.047
			5.1055	0.052				5.2462	0.051
			4.6509	0.091				4.6231	0.097
			4.4945	0.101				4.5077	0.100
5	3	3	7.0788	0.009	5	5	3	7.5780	0.010
			6.9818	0.011				7.5429	0.010
			5.6485	0.049				5.7055	0.046
			5.5152	0.051				5.6264	0.051
			4.5333	0.097				4.5451	0.100
			4.4121	0.109				4.5363	0.102
5	4	1	6.9545	0.008	5	5	4	7.8229	0.010
			6.8400	0.011				7.7914	0.010
			4.9855	0.044				5.6657	0.049
			4.8600	0.056				5.6429	0.050
			3.9873	0.098				4.5229	0.099
			3.9600	0.102				4.5200	0.101
5	4	2	7.2045	0.009	5	5	5	8.0000	0.009
			7.1182	0.010				7.9800	0.010
			5.2727	0.049				5.7800	0.049
			5.2682	0.050				5.6600	0.051
			4.5409	0.098				4.5600	0.100
			4.5182	0.101				4.5000	0.102

Table F Critical values of χ^2 at various levels of probability (chi-square)

For any particular *df* the observed value of χ^2 is significant at a given level of significance if it is *equal to* or *larger than* the critical values shown in the table.

df	0.10	0.05	0.02	0.01	0.001
1	2.71	3.84	5.41	6.64	10.83
2	4.60	5.99	7.82	9.21	13.82
3	6.25	7.82	9.84	11.34	16.27
4	7.78	9.49	11.67	13.28	18.46
5	9.24	11.07	13.39	15.09	20.52
6	10.64	12.59	15.03	16.81	22.46
7	12.02	14.07	16.62	18.48	24.32
8	13.36	15.51	18.17	20.09	26.12
9	14.68	16.92	19.68	21.67	27.88
10	15.99	18.31	21.16	23.21	29.59
11	17.28	19.68	22.62	24.72	31.26
12	18.55	21.03	24.05	26.22	32.91
13	19.81	22.36	25.47	27.69	34.53
14	21.06	23.68	26.87	29.14	36.12
15	22.31	25.00	28.26	30.58	37.70
16	23.54	26.30	29.63	32.00	39.29
17	24.77	27.59	31.00	33.41	40.75
18	25.99	28.87	32.35	34.80	42.31
19	27.20	30.14	33.69	36.19	43.82
20	28.41	31.41	35.02	37.57	45.32
21	29.62	32.67	36.34	38.93	46.80
22	30.81	33.92	37.66	40.29	48.27
23	32.01	35.17	38.97	41.64	49.73
24	33.20	36.42	40.27	42.98	51.18
25	34.38	37.65	41.57	44.31	52.62
26	35.56	38.88	42.86	45.64	54.05
27	36.74	40.11	44.14	46.97	55.48
28	37.92	41.34	45.42	48.28	56.89
29	39.09	42.56	46.69	49.59	58.30
30	40.26	43.77	47.96	50.89	59.70

Table G Critical values of S (one-tailed) at various levels of probability (Jonckheere trend)

For any C and n the observed value of S is significant at a given level of significance if it is *equal to* or *larger than* the critical values shown in the table.

Significance level $p < 0.05$

				n					
C	2	3	4	5	6	7	8	9	10
3	10	17	24	33	42	53	64	76	88
4	14	26	38	51	66	82	100	118	138
5	20	34	51	71	92	115	140	166	194
6	26	44	67	93	121	151	184	219	256

Significance level $p < 0.01$

3	–	23	32	45	59	74	90	106	124
4	20	34	50	71	92	115	140	167	195
5	26	48	72	99	129	162	197	234	274
6	34	62	94	130	170	213	260	309	361

Appendix 2: Statistical tables

Table H   Critical values of r_S at various levels of probability
(Spearman rank correlation coefficient)

For any N the observed value of r_S is significant at a given level of significance
if it is *equal to* or *larger than* the critical values shown in the table.

	Level of significance for one-tailed test			
	0.05	*0.025*	*0.01*	*0.005*
N	*Level of significance for two-tailed test*			
(number of				
subjects)	*0.10*	*0.05*	*0.02*	*0.01*
5	0.900	1.000	1.000	–
6	0.829	0.886	0.943	1.000
7	0.714	0.786	0.893	0.929
8	0.643	0.738	0.833	0.881
9	0.600	0.683	0.783	0.833
10	0.564	0.648	0.746	0.794
12	0.506	0.591	0.712	0.777
14	0.456	0.544	0.645	0.715
16	0.425	0.506	0.601	0.665
18	0.399	0.475	0.564	0.625
20	0.377	0.450	0.534	0.591
22	0.359	0.428	0.508	0.562
24	0.343	0.409	0.485	0.537
26	0.329	0.392	0.465	0.515
28	0.317	0.377	0.448	0.496
30	0.306	0.364	0.432	0.478

N.B. When the required value of N is not shown use the next lowest number.

Table I Critical values of *t* at various levels of probability (*t* test)

For any particular *df* the observed value of *t* is significant at a given level of significance if it is *equal to* or *larger than* the critical values shown in the table.

df	Level of significance for one-tailed test					
	0.10	0.05	0.025	0.01	0.005	0.0005
	Level of significance for two-tailed test					
	0.20	0.10	0.05	0.02	0.01	0.001
1	3.078	6.314	12.706	31.821	63.657	636.619
2	1.886	2.920	4.303	6.965	9.925	31.598
3	1.638	2.353	3.182	4.541	5.841	12.941
4	1.533	2.132	2.776	3.747	4.604	8.610
5	1.476	2.015	2.571	3.365	4.032	6.859
6	1.440	1.943	2.447	3.143	3.707	5.959
7	1.415	1.895	2.365	2.998	3.499	5.405
8	1.397	1.860	2.306	2.896	3.355	5.041
9	1.383	1.833	2.262	2.821	3.250	4.781
10	1.372	1.812	2.228	2.764	3.169	4.587
11	1.363	1.796	2.201	2.718	3.106	4.437
12	1.356	1.782	2.179	2.681	3.055	4.318
13	1.350	1.771	2.160	2.650	3.012	4.221
14	1.345	1.761	2.145	2.624	2.977	4.140
15	1.341	1.753	2.131	2.602	2.947	4.073
16	1.337	1.746	2.120	2.583	2.921	4.015
17	1.333	1.740	2.110	2.567	2.898	3.965
18	1.330	1.734	2.101	2.552	2.878	3.922
19	1.328	1.729	2.093	2.539	2.861	3.883
20	1.325	1.725	2.086	2.528	2.845	3.850
21	1.323	1.721	2.080	2.518	2.831	3.819
22	1.321	1.717	2.074	2.508	2.819	3.792
23	1.319	1.714	2.069	2.500	2.807	3.767
24	1.318	1.711	2.064	2.492	2.797	3.745
25	1.316	1.708	2.060	2.485	2.787	3.725
26	1.315	1.706	2.056	2.479	2.779	3.707
27	1.314	1.703	2.052	2.473	2.771	3.690
28	1.313	1.701	2.048	2.467	2.763	3.674
29	1.311	1.699	2.045	2.462	2.756	3.659
30	1.310	1.697	2.042	2.457	2.750	3.646
40	1.303	1.684	2.021	2.423	2.704	3.551
60	1.296	1.671	2.000	2.390	2.660	3.460
120	1.289	1.658	1.980	2.358	2.617	3.373
∞	1.282	1.645	1.960	2.326	2.576	3.291

N.B. When required *df* is not shown use the next lowest number, except for very large *df*s (well over 120), when you can use the row for infinity (∞).

Table J Critical values of F at various levels of probability (F ratios)

For any v_1 and v_2 the observed value of F is significant at a given level of significance if it is *equal to* or *larger than* the critical values shown in Tables J(1)–J(4).

Table J(1) Critical values of F at $p < 0.05$

v_2	v_1											
	1	2	3	4	5	6	7	8	10	12	24	∞
1	161.4	199.5	215.7	224.6	230.2	234.0	236.8	238.9	241.9	243.9	249.0	254.3
2	18.5	19.0	19.2	19.2	19.3	19.3	19.4	19.4	19.4	19.4	19.5	19.5
3	10.13	9.55	9.28	9.12	9.01	8.94	8.89	8.85	8.79	8.74	8.64	8.53
4	7.71	6.94	6.59	6.39	6.26	6.16	6.09	6.04	5.96	5.91	5.77	5.63
5	6.61	5.79	5.41	5.19	5.05	4.95	4.88	4.82	4.74	4.68	4.53	4.36
6	5.99	5.14	4.76	4.53	4.39	4.28	4.21	4.15	4.06	4.00	3.84	3.67
7	5.59	4.74	4.35	4.12	3.97	3.87	3.79	3.73	3.64	3.57	3.41	3.23
8	5.32	4.46	4.07	3.84	3.69	3.58	3.50	3.44	3.35	3.28	3.12	2.93
9	5.12	4.26	3.86	3.63	3.48	3.37	3.29	3.23	3.14	3.07	2.90	2.71
10	4.96	4.10	3.71	3.48	3.33	3.22	3.14	3.07	2.98	2.91	2.74	2.54
11	4.84	3.98	3.59	3.36	3.20	3.09	3.01	2.95	2.85	2.79	2.61	2.40
12	4.75	3.89	3.49	3.26	3.11	3.00	2.91	2.85	2.75	2.69	2.51	2.30
13	4.67	3.81	3.41	3.18	3.03	2.92	2.83	2.77	2.67	2.60	2.42	2.21
14	4.60	3.74	3.34	3.11	2.96	2.85	2.76	2.70	2.60	2.53	2.35	2.13
15	4.54	3.68	3.29	3.06	2.90	2.79	2.71	2.64	2.54	2.48	2.29	2.07
16	4.49	3.63	3.24	3.01	2.85	2.74	2.66	2.59	2.49	2.42	2.24	2.01
17	4.45	3.59	3.20	2.96	2.81	2.70	2.61	2.55	2.45	2.38	2.19	1.96
18	4.41	3.55	3.16	2.93	2.77	2.66	2.58	2.51	2.41	2.34	2.15	1.92
19	4.38	3.52	3.13	2.90	2.74	2.63	2.54	2.48	2.38	2.31	2.11	1.88
20	4.35	3.49	3.10	2.87	2.71	2.60	2.51	2.45	2.35	2.28	2.08	1.84
21	4.32	3.47	3.07	2.84	2.68	2.57	2.49	2.42	2.32	2.25	2.05	1.81
22	4.30	3.44	3.05	2.82	2.66	2.55	2.46	2.40	2.30	2.23	2.03	1.78
23	4.28	3.42	3.03	2.80	2.64	2.53	2.44	2.37	2.27	2.20	2.00	1.76
24	4.26	3.40	3.01	2.78	2.62	2.51	2.42	2.36	2.25	2.18	1.98	1.73
25	4.24	3.39	2.99	2.76	2.60	2.49	2.40	2.34	2.24	2.16	1.96	1.71
26	4.23	3.37	2.98	2.74	2.59	2.47	2.39	2.32	2.22	2.15	1.95	1.69
27	4.21	3.35	2.96	2.73	2.57	2.46	2.37	2.31	2.20	2.13	1.93	1.67
28	4.20	3.34	2.95	2.71	2.56	2.45	2.36	2.29	2.19	2.12	1.91	1.65
29	4.18	3.33	2.93	2.70	2.55	2.43	2.35	2.28	2.18	2.10	1.90	1.64
30	4.17	3.32	2.92	2.69	2.53	2.42	2.33	2.27	2.16	2.09	1.89	1.62
32	4.15	3.29	2.90	2.67	2.51	2.40	2.31	2.24	2.14	2.07	1.86	1.59
34	4.13	3.28	2.88	2.65	2.49	2.38	2.29	2.23	2.12	2.05	1.84	1.57
36	4.11	3.26	2.87	2.63	2.48	2.36	2.28	2.21	2.11	2.03	1.82	1.55
38	4.10	3.24	2.85	2.62	2.46	2.35	2.26	2.19	2.09	2.02	1.81	1.53
40	4.08	3.23	2.84	2.61	2.45	2.34	2.25	2.18	2.08	2.00	1.79	1.51
60	4.00	3.15	2.76	2.53	2.37	2.25	2.17	2.10	1.99	1.92	1.70	1.39
120	3.92	3.07	2.68	2.45	2.29	2.18	2.09	2.02	1.91	1.83	1.61	1.25
∞	3.84	3.00	2.60	2.37	2.21	2.10	2.01	1.94	1.83	1.75	1.52	1.00

N.B. When the required *df*s are not shown use the next lowest number. For very large *df*s (well over 120) you can use infinity (∞).

Table J(2) Critical values of F at $p < 0.025$

v_2	\multicolumn{11}{c}{v_1}

v_2	1	2	3	4	5	6	7	8	10	12	24	∞
1	648	800	864	900	922	937	948	957	969	977	997	1018
2	38.5	39.0	39.2	39.2	39.3	39.3	39.4	39.4	39.4	39.4	39.5	39.5
3	17.4	16.0	15.4	15.1	14.9	14.7	14.6	14.5	14.4	14.3	14.1	13.9
4	12.22	10.65	9.98	9.60	9.36	9.20	9.07	8.98	8.84	8.75	8.51	8.26
5	10.01	8.43	7.76	7.39	7.15	6.98	6.85	6.76	6.62	6.52	6.28	6.02
6	8.81	7.26	6.60	6.23	5.99	5.82	5.70	5.60	5.46	5.37	5.12	4.85
7	8.07	6.54	5.89	5.52	5.29	5.12	4.99	4.90	4.76	4.67	4.42	4.14
8	7.57	6.06	5.42	5.05	4.82	4.65	4.53	4.43	4.30	4.20	3.95	3.67
9	7.21	5.71	5.08	4.72	4.48	4.32	4.20	4.10	3.96	3.87	3.61	3.33
10	6.94	5.46	4.83	4.47	4.24	4.07	3.95	3.85	3.72	3.62	3.37	3.08
11	6.72	5.26	4.63	4.28	4.04	3.88	3.76	3.66	3.53	3.43	3.17	2.88
12	6.55	5.10	4.47	4.12	3.89	3.73	3.61	3.51	3.37	3.28	3.02	2.72
13	6.41	4.97	4.35	4.00	3.77	3.60	3.48	3.39	3.25	3.15	2.89	2.60
14	6.30	4.86	4.24	3.89	3.66	3.50	3.38	3.29	3.15	3.05	2.79	2.49
15	6.20	4.76	4.15	3.80	3.58	3.41	3.29	3.20	3.06	2.96	2.70	2.40
16	6.12	4.69	4.08	3.73	3.50	3.34	3.22	3.12	2.99	2.89	2.63	2.32
17	6.04	4.62	4.01	3.66	3.44	3.28	3.16	3.06	2.92	2.82	2.56	2.25
18	5.98	4.56	3.95	3.61	3.38	3.22	3.10	3.01	2.87	2.77	2.50	2.19
19	5.92	4.51	3.90	3.56	3.33	3.17	3.05	2.96	2.82	2.72	2.45	2.13
20	5.87	4.46	3.86	3.51	3.29	3.13	3.01	2.91	2.77	2.68	2.41	2.09
21	5.83	4.42	3.82	3.48	3.25	3.09	2.97	2.87	2.73	2.64	2.37	2.04
22	5.79	4.38	3.78	3.44	3.22	3.05	2.93	2.84	2.70	2.60	2.33	2.00
23	5.75	4.35	3.75	3.41	3.18	3.02	2.90	2.81	2.67	2.57	2.30	1.97
24	5.72	4.32	3.72	3.38	3.15	2.99	2.87	2.78	2.64	2.54	2.27	1.94
25	5.69	4.29	3.69	3.35	3.13	2.97	2.85	2.75	2.61	2.51	2.24	1.91
26	5.66	4.27	3.67	3.33	3.10	2.94	2.82	2.73	2.59	2.49	2.22	1.88
27	5.63	4.24	3.65	3.31	3.08	2.92	2.80	2.71	2.57	2.47	2.19	1.85
28	5.61	4.22	3.63	3.29	3.06	2.90	2.78	2.69	2.55	2.45	2.17	1.83
29	5.59	4.20	3.61	3.27	3.04	2.88	2.76	2.67	2.53	2.43	2.15	1.81
30	5.57	4.18	3.59	3.25	3.03	2.87	2.75	2.65	2.51	2.41	2.14	1.79
32	5.53	4.15	3.56	3.22	3.00	2.84	2.72	2.62	2.48	2.38	2.10	1.75
34	5.50	4.12	3.53	3.19	2.97	2.81	2.69	2.59	2.45	2.35	2.08	1.72
36	5.47	4.09	3.51	3.17	2.94	2.79	2.66	2.57	2.43	2.33	2.05	1.69
38	5.45	4.07	3.48	3.15	2.92	2.76	2.64	2.55	2.41	2.31	2.03	1.66
40	5.42	4.05	3.46	3.13	2.90	2.74	2.62	2.53	2.39	2.29	2.01	1.64
60	5.29	3.93	3.34	3.01	2.79	2.63	2.51	2.41	2.27	2.17	1.88	1.48
120	5.15	3.80	3.23	2.89	2.67	2.52	2.39	2.30	2.16	2.05	1.76	1.31
∞	5.02	3.69	3.12	2.79	2.57	2.41	2.29	2.19	2.05	1.94	1.64	1.00

Table J(3)   Critical values of F at $p < 0.01$

v_2	1	2	3	4	5	6	7	8	10	12	24	∞
1	4052	5000	5403	5625	5764	5859	5928	5981	6056	6106	6235	6366
2	98.5	99.0	99.2	99.2	99.3	99.3	99.4	99.4	99.4	99.4	99.5	99.5
3	34.1	30.8	29.5	28.7	28.2	27.9	27.7	27.5	27.2	27.1	26.6	26.1
4	21.2	18.0	16.7	16.0	15.5	15.2	15.0	14.8	14.5	14.4	13.9	13.5
5	16.26	13.27	12.06	11.39	10.97	10.67	10.46	10.29	10.05	9.89	9.47	9.02
6	13.74	10.92	9.78	9.15	8.75	8.47	8.26	8.10	7.87	7.72	7.31	6.88
7	12.25	9.55	8.45	7.85	7.46	7.19	6.99	6.84	6.62	6.47	6.07	5.65
8	11.26	8.65	7.59	7.01	6.63	6.37	6.18	6.03	5.81	5.67	5.28	4.86
9	10.56	8.02	6.99	6.42	6.06	5.80	5.61	5.47	5.26	5.11	4.73	4.31
10	10.04	7.56	6.55	5.99	5.64	5.39	5.20	5.06	4.85	4.71	4.33	3.91
11	9.65	7.21	6.22	5.67	5.32	5.07	4.89	4.74	4.54	4.40	4.02	3.60
12	9.33	6.93	5.95	5.41	5.06	4.82	4.64	4.50	4.30	4.16	3.78	3.36
13	9.07	6.70	5.74	5.21	4.86	4.62	4.44	4.30	4.10	3.96	3.59	3.17
14	8.86	6.51	5.56	5.04	4.70	4.46	4.28	4.14	3.94	3.80	3.43	3.00
15	8.68	6.36	5.42	4.89	4.56	4.32	4.14	4.00	3.80	3.67	3.29	2.87
16	8.53	6.23	5.29	4.77	4.44	4.20	4.03	3.89	3.69	3.55	3.18	2.75
17	8.40	6.11	5.18	4.67	4.34	4.10	3.93	3.79	3.59	3.46	3.08	2.65
18	8.29	6.01	5.09	4.58	4.25	4.01	3.84	3.71	3.51	3.37	3.00	2.57
19	8.18	5.93	5.01	4.50	4.17	3.94	3.77	3.63	3.43	3.30	2.92	2.49
20	8.10	5.85	4.94	4.43	4.10	3.87	3.70	3.56	3.37	3.23	2.86	2.42
21	8.02	5.78	4.87	4.37	4.04	3.81	3.64	3.51	3.31	3.17	2.80	2.36
22	7.95	5.72	4.82	4.31	3.99	3.76	3.59	3.45	3.26	3.12	2.75	2.31
23	7.88	5.66	4.76	4.26	3.94	3.71	3.54	3.41	3.21	3.07	2.70	2.26
24	7.82	5.61	4.72	4.22	3.90	3.67	3.50	3.36	3.17	3.03	2.66	2.21
25	7.77	5.57	4.68	4.18	3.86	3.63	3.46	3.32	3.13	2.99	2.62	2.17
26	7.72	5.53	4.64	4.14	3.82	3.59	3.42	3.29	3.09	2.96	2.58	2.13
27	7.68	5.49	4.60	4.11	3.78	3.56	3.39	3.26	3.06	2.93	2.55	2.10
28	7.64	5.45	4.57	4.07	3.75	3.53	3.36	3.23	3.03	2.90	2.52	2.06
29	7.60	5.42	4.54	4.04	3.73	3.50	3.33	3.20	3.00	2.87	2.49	2.03
30	7.56	5.39	4.51	4.02	3.70	3.47	3.30	3.17	2.98	2.84	2.47	2.01
32	7.50	5.34	4.46	3.97	3.65	3.43	3.26	3.13	2.93	2.80	2.42	1.96
34	7.45	5.29	4.42	3.93	3.61	3.39	3.22	3.09	2.90	2.76	2.38	1.91
36	7.40	5.25	4.38	3.89	3.58	3.35	3.18	3.05	2.86	2.72	2.35	1.87
38	7.35	5.21	4.34	3.86	3.54	3.32	3.15	3.02	2.83	2.69	2.32	1.84
40	7.31	5.18	4.31	3.83	3.51	3.29	3.12	2.99	2.80	2.66	2.29	1.80
60	7.08	4.98	4.13	3.65	3.34	3.12	2.95	2.82	2.63	2.50	2.12	1.60
120	6.85	4.79	3.95	3.48	3.17	2.96	2.79	2.66	2.47	2.34	1.95	1.38
∞	6.63	4.61	3.78	3.32	3.02	2.80	2.64	2.51	2.32	2.18	1.79	1.00

Table J(4)   Critical values of F at $p < 0.001$

v_2	1	2	3	4	5	6	7	8	10	12	24	∞
1*	4053	5000	5404	5625	5764	5859	5929	5981	6056	6107	6235	6366
2	998.5	999.0	999.2	999.2	999.3	999.3	999.4	999.4	999.4	999.4	999.5	999.5
3	167.0	148.5	141.1	137.1	134.6	132.8	131.5	130.6	129.2	128.3	125.9	123.5
4	74.14	61.25	56.18	53.44	51.71	50.53	49.66	49.00	48.05	47.41	45.77	44.05
5	47.18	37.12	33.20	31.09	29.75	28.83	28.16	27.65	26.92	26.42	25.14	23.79
6	35.51	27.00	23.70	21.92	20.80	20.03	19.46	19.03	18.41	17.99	16.90	15.75
7	29.25	21.69	18.77	17.20	16.21	15.52	15.02	14.63	14.08	13.71	12.73	11.70
8	25.42	18.49	15.83	14.39	13.48	12.86	12.40	12.05	11.54	11.19	10.30	9.34
9	22.86	16.39	13.90	12.56	11.71	11.13	10.69	10.37	9.87	9.57	8.72	7.81
10	21.04	14.91	12.55	11.28	10.48	9.93	9.52	9.20	8.74	8.44	7.64	6.76
11	19.69	13.81	11.56	10.35	9.58	9.05	8.66	8.35	7.92	7.63	6.85	6.00
12	18.64	12.97	10.80	9.63	8.89	8.38	8.00	7.71	7.29	7.00	6.25	5.42
13	17.82	12.31	10.21	9.07	8.35	7.86	7.49	7.21	6.80	6.52	5.78	4.97
14	17.14	11.78	9.73	8.62	7.92	7.44	7.08	6.80	6.40	6.13	5.41	4.60
15	16.59	11.34	9.34	8.25	7.57	7.09	6.74	6.47	6.08	5.81	5.10	4.31
16	16.12	10.97	9.01	7.94	7.27	6.80	6.46	6.19	5.81	5.55	4.85	4.06
17	15.72	10.66	8.73	7.68	7.02	6.56	6.22	5.96	5.58	5.32	4.63	3.85
18	15.38	10.39	8.49	7.46	6.81	6.35	6.02	5.76	5.39	5.13	4.45	3.67
19	15.08	10.16	8.28	7.27	6.62	6.18	5.85	5.59	5.22	4.97	4.29	3.51
20	14.82	9.95	8.10	7.10	6.46	6.02	5.69	5.44	5.08	4.82	4.15	3.38
21	14.59	9.77	7.94	6.95	6.32	5.88	5.56	5.31	4.95	4.70	4.03	3.26
22	14.38	9.61	7.80	6.81	6.19	5.76	5.44	5.19	4.83	4.58	3.92	3.15
23	14.19	9.47	7.67	6.70	6.08	5.65	5.33	5.09	4.73	4.48	3.82	3.05
24	14.03	9.34	7.55	6.59	5.98	5.55	5.23	4.99	4.64	4.39	3.74	2.97
25	13.88	9.22	7.45	6.49	5.89	5.46	5.15	4.91	4.56	4.31	3.66	2.89
26	13.74	9.12	7.36	6.41	5.80	5.38	5.07	4.83	4.48	4.24	3.59	2.82
27	13.61	9.02	7.27	6.33	5.73	5.31	5.00	4.76	4.41	4.17	3.52	2.75
28	13.50	8.93	7.19	6.25	5.66	5.24	4.93	4.69	4.35	4.11	3.46	2.69
29	13.39	8.85	7.12	6.19	5.59	5.18	4.87	4.64	4.29	4.05	3.41	2.64
30	13.29	8.77	7.05	6.12	5.53	5.12	4.82	4.58	4.24	4.00	3.36	2.59
32	13.12	8.64	6.94	6.01	5.43	5.02	4.72	4.48	4.14	3.91	3.27	2.50
34	12.97	8.52	6.83	5.92	5.34	4.93	4.63	4.40	4.06	3.83	3.19	2.42
36	12.83	8.42	6.74	5.84	5.26	4.86	4.56	4.33	3.99	3.76	3.12	2.35
38	12.71	8.33	6.66	5.76	5.19	4.79	4.49	4.26	3.93	3.70	3.06	2.29
40	12.61	8.25	6.59	5.70	5.13	4.73	4.44	4.21	3.87	3.64	3.01	2.23
60	11.97	7.77	6.17	5.31	4.76	4.37	4.09	3.86	3.54	3.32	2.69	1.89
120	11.38	7.32	5.78	4.95	4.42	4.04	3.77	3.55	3.24	3.02	2.40	1.54
∞	10.83	6.91	5.42	4.62	4.10	3.74	3.47	3.27	2.96	2.74	2.13	1.00

*Entries for $v_2 = 1$ must be multiplied by 100.

Index